Also by Raymond B. Flannery, Jr., Ph.D.

*Becoming Stress-Resistant*
*through the Project SMART Program*

*Post-Traumatic Stress Disorder:*
*The Victim's Guide to Healing and Recovery*

*Violence in the Workplace*

# RAYMOND B. FLANNERY, JR., PH.D.

# VIOLENCE IN AMERICA

Coping with Drugs,
Distressed Families,
Inadequate Schooling,
and Acts of Hate

CONTINUUM I NEW YORK

1998
The Continuum Publishing Company
370 Lexington Avenue, New York, NY 10017

Copyright © 1997 by Raymond B. Flannery, Jr.

All rights reserved. No part of this book may be reproduced,
stored in a retrieval system, or transmitted in any form or
by any means, electronic, mechanical, photocopying, recording,
or otherwise, without the written permission of
The Continuum Publishing Company.

Printed in the United States of America

**Library Of Congress Catalog-in-Publication Data**

Flannery, Raymond B.
  Violence in America : coping with drugs, distressed families,
inadequate schooling, and acts of hate / Raymond B. Flannery, Jr.
    p.   cm.
  Includes bibliographical references and index.
  ISBN 0-8264-1002-2 (hardcover : alk. Paper)
    1. Violence. 2. Violence—United States. 3. Violence—United
States—Prevention. 4. Social values—United States. I. Title.
RC569.5.V55F56 1997
155.9'2—dc21                                              96-40431
                                                             CIP

For Thomas M. Garrett, Ph.D.,
and
Elizabeth L. Lomke

WITHDRAWN

JUL -- 1999

# Contents

# Preface

It is unlikely that any American reading these words has been left untouched by violence, either as a victim of a direct malicious act, as a family member or friend of someone who has been a victim, or as a witness to crime and violence.

While the end of the Cold War reduced the external threat of nuclear attack, the internal threat of crime and violence remains at unacceptably high levels. There are no longer any safe havens at home. Homicide, terrorism, torture, rape, assault, robbery, fraud, embezzlement, and other acts of aggression have become so pervasive that most Americans now cite violence as one of their major concerns. Violence in America has become a national public health problem.

For over twenty-five years, I have been counseling the victims of these acts of hatred, many suffering from the effects of Post-Traumatic Stress Disorder (PTSD). I have seen firsthand the human suffering, medical expense, and lost productivity that such acts may create in their aftermath. For these same twenty-five years, as a citizen, I have watched with equal alarm the increasing rates of crime and violence in the nation.

Although I have learned something about the nature of the perpetrators of these acts from their victims, given the national increase in crime, I felt it important, as a professional and as a concerned citizen, to learn more about why this increase was occurring. I went in search of a book for the general reader, as well as the professional, which would help in understanding the risk factors that contribute to violence and what could be done to contain and possibly prevent it. I could find no such book. Although I located several scholarly and technical studies on violence in the various medical and behavioral science disciplines, these articles were highly specialized and addressed only one aspect of the problem. Each scientist and each laboratory tended to work in isolation. There was no comprehensive guide for this topic of urgent national importance.

This book is the first to attempt to address this need by reviewing the latest findings on the risk factors that may result in violence (part 1) and then outlining current, successful programs to contain and cutail such mayhem (part 2). In this book, I have chosen those theories, research findings, and intervention approaches that appear to be the most robust.

Currently, there is no known way to predict violence with one hundred percent accuracy. Observers of violence speak of risk factors, factors that increase the probability of an aggressive outburst in some persons. All things being equal, the greater the number of risk factors that are present, the greater the possibility of violence. Since violence has many differing risk factors, many of which interact with one another, and since there is no single cause for the current national epidemic of violence, we will need to examine the various possible roots for this problem.

Intensive reading across disciplines, study, and observation have led me to the following understanding of violence in America. In each generation there are common cultural, biological, sociological, and psychological risk factors for crime and violence. For the most part, these potentials for violence are held in check by our societal institutions: business, government, the family, school, and religion. These institutions create caring attachments among us, provide socially acceptable guidelines for how we should interact with each other, and strengthen the sense of community in the process.

When society undergoes a radical transformation, these social institutions are altered and must themselves adapt to the changing times. These dislocations produce confusion, or *anomie*, in how we are to behave, disrupt our caring attachments to one another, weaken our sense of community, and exacerbate the risk factors for crime that would otherwise be held in check to a greater degree. This happened in our country in the period from 1880 to the 1890s, when society underwent a major social shift during the emergence of the industrial state and when the levels of crime increased substantially.

We are now in another major period of social change as we move from the industrial state with its emphasis on the production of goods to the postindustrial state with its emphasis on knowledge. This upheaval is forcing our societal institutions to change and is disrupting our caring attachments. The guidelines for how we should relate to each other in socially cohesive ways are changing. At the present moment in this evolution, there is an overemphasis on personal entitlement, material gain, and instant gratification with less emphasis on responsibilities to others and to community. These cultural changes appear to have exacerbated the biological, sociological, and psychological risk factors for violence, and violent crime has increased just as it did during the earlier period in our history that we have noted.

Not all of the news is discouraging, however. In fact, the message of this book is one of hope. When an epidemic of crime occurred earlier in our history, concerned citizens developed successful strategies to contain that crime and reduce its risk. Similarly, in today's age, citizens have begun to address our national public health crisis of violent behavior, and many of their effective approaches for restoring community are presented in these pages. The framework for understanding our current levels of violence permits us to develop more focused solutions to the causes of violent crime and to understand how the individual's approach fits into the larger solution to this multidetermined problem. The strategies presented here for coping are neither politically liberal nor conservative. Rather they reflect practical approaches that appear effective and affordable.

Finding creative solutions in the face of adversity has been one of our strengths. To reduce the level of violence in America will require the efforts of each one of us, but our resolve is no less than that of our forebears. Together, we can stop the violence. This overview on the causes of violence and how to reduce their risk offers us one place from which to begin.

An author's intellectual roots are many and diverse. I would like to thank my patients and students who have taught me much about violence in America, the several members of the Assaulted Staff Action Program, and the science community that continues to work quietly to unravel the unknowns of violence. I want to pay special thanks to the following persons who have provided important academic, clinical, or administrative support: Paul Appelbaum, M.D.; Paul Barreira, M.D.; Joseph Coyle, M.D.; Robert Dorwart, M.D.; Wallace Haley, Jr., M.D.; Walter Penk, Ph.D.; Mollie Schoenberg; Marylou Sudders, LICSW; and James Woods, S.J., Ed.D. I have been especially fortunate in having many of the same team as I had for my first three books. Gene Gollogly, Ulla Schnell, and Evander Lomke, at Continuum; Norma Robbins, who has again typed the manuscript; and my wife Georgina, who has served as librarian, researcher, and indexer for various aspects of the current project. These men and women have offered wise counsel and advice, but any errors remain my sole responsibility.

This book is dedicated equally to Thomas M. Garrett, Ph.D., and Elizabeth L. Lomke. Dr. Garrett has been a colleague, mentor, and friend, and has taught me much about human behavior, including violence, over the years. Elizabeth Lomke has taught a good many of us about the importance of caring attachments in the face of life's adversities.

Raymond B. Flannery, Jr., Ph.D.
Autumn, 1996

# Author's Note
## and Editorial Method

Violence in America with its often co-occurring psychological trauma, is a rapidly expanding area of scientific and medical inquiry. General guidelines are presented here, but citizens, organizations, and companies who desire to address some aspect of violence are advised to consider the latest research findings and any laws or policies that may govern the programs they may wish to implement. Consideration should also be given to hiring specialists in legal matters, security analysis, liability issues, and victim debriefing for specific organizational goals, if need be. With respect to the possible aftermath of violence—psychological trauma and Post-Traumatic Stress Disorder—medicine and other forms of treatment are constantly being upgraded and improved. This book is not intended to be a substitute for the advice of your physician or professional counselor. Raise any questions that you may have with them, and always follow the advice of your physician or counselor first.

· · ·

The Select Readings list and Appendix A, which have been provided at the end of the volume, also contain all of the citations noted in the book.

· · ·

All of the examples in this book are real events that have happened to victims of violent acts. Identifying information has been deleted to the extent that this has been possible.

# PART ONE

# VIOLENCE IN AMERICA: CAUSES

# 1

# IT'S THE NATURE OF THE TIMES: CULTURAL FACTORS IN VIOLENCE

*Cain rose up against his brother Abel and killed him.*
— Genesis 4:8

*We are all in the same boat, in a stormy sea . . . .*
— G. K. Chesterton

*Dateline: San Francisco, California. July 1, 1993.*

The apartment was empty. Eviction notices were posted. The sense of failure seared one's soul. A moment of shattered glass also seared the soul of ten-month-old Catherine. . . .

The dream had begun earnestly enough ten years before. The would-be speculator had the California dream of making his fortune in real estate, and the attorneys of one of the city's best law firms had helped him broker his first deal for mobile trailer parks in Indiana and Kentucky. The world was his for the taking.

A decade of real estate deals attempted and failed had passed, including three recent forays in Las Vegas. The downward spiral had been slow and continuous, and a recent recession had brought financial ruin. Charges of fraud by former investors. Unpaid taxes. Unpaid rent. Nine dollars in his checking account precluded his declaring personal bankruptcy.

On this pleasant Thursday afternoon, the failed speculator, dressed in suit and tie, packed his briefcase with two nine-millimeter semiautomatic pistols, a forty-five caliber automatic handgun, several rounds of ammunition. Included also were his four-page letter with its charges of being "raped" by advisors and the names of the fifty people who had to pay for this bad advice.

Arriving in the business district, this neat, polite, fifty-five-year-old man, who had abhorred violence all his life, quietly rode the elevator to the thirty-fourth floor, the law offices of the firm that had helped him get his start. When the doors opened, he was calm and expressionless as he turned to the right, walked to a glass-enclosed disposition room, and opened fire. Catherine's mother was one of the first to die in the shattered glass. Another was the law firm's senior partner.

He marched down to the thirty-third floor where he met a young married couple. Inseparable since college, they would now be inseparable in death. The husband shielded his wife and was fatally wounded.

The thirty-second floor.

The thirty-first floor.

The thirtieth floor.

So it went until, in the stairwell of the twenty-ninth floor, the gunman shot himself to death as the police charged toward him.

Amid the anguished echoes of the first-floor atrium that now served as a field hospital, the toll was assessed: eight dead, six wounded, and hundreds terrified and grieving.

For fifteen long, terrifying, and ugly minutes, the world had been his for the taking. The sense of failure seared one's soul.

The United States is a violent country. Episodes of violent crime, like this one in San Francisco, are not exceptions to the rule. Indeed, comparative statistics among nations (Dobrin, Wiersema, Loftin, and McDowall, 1996) indicate that the United States outranks most other nations of the industrial world in violent crimes like assault, rape, and robbery. In the category of murder, we are far and away the most violent industrialized nation on earth. Consider the following informal national survey of homicides drawn at random.

- Waterville, Maine—Two elderly nuns are murdered in their convent by a thirty-seven-year-old male.
- Boston, Massachusetts—A sixty-one-year-old free-lance photographer sells photos to a newspaper of a fatal accident scene. Ten days later he is charged with running over one of the victims.
- New York, New York—A twenty-seven-year-old female health aide beats two elderly women to death for their money.
- Toledo, Ohio—A fifteen-year-old boy kills his sixty-two-year-old foster mother with a hatchet and sets her on fire because she would not allow him to keep a stray dog.

- Chicago, Illinois—A young, pregnant mother of three is murdered by her former boyfriend, who extracts the fetus from the deceased mother to take as his own child.
- York, Nebraska—A fifty-seven-year-old woman is sexually assaulted, and then her attacker runs over her in a car, shortly before Christmas.
- Salt Lake City, Utah—A ninth-grade male student hijacks a school bus, shoots the driver, and commits suicide.
- Portland, Oregon—A ten-year-old boy pleads guilty to manslaughter in the death of his five-year-old sister, who would not go to her room as he directed.

This prohibitive murder rate, in addition to the other unacceptably high levels of violent crime, is creating a nation of anxious and demoralized citizens who feel angry at being captives of this violence and at being helpless to stop it.

Many live in houses with extra locks on the doors and a perimeter security system around their homes, similar antitheft devices on their vehicles, and an attack dog for company. They go to work furtively to avoid being mugged in transit and enter worksites that require special-issue surveillance cards to gain access. Even within the building they have to lock up personal possessions to avoid theft. At home again in the evening, the televised news offers no respite. A plane is downed by a terrorist on a routine flight. A mother calmly drowns her young children because she did not like them. Should one go for a walk in the evening air to calm down? Few are the souls that would venture forth in their neighborhoods after dark. Better to wait until daylight when you might be able to escape or at least obtain a description of your assailant. They may be told that crime is decreasing, but it does not make them any less anxious. In some ways, they have become prisoners of affluence.

How has it come to this? What are we to make of any of these acts of violence? How are we to understand the massacre in the San Francisco office tower or the mother who destroys her own children? Are these assailants out of their minds? Are they on drugs? Are they hopeless victims of some social ill? More importantly, can we do anything to stop this national crime spree or are we helpless in the face of this madness?

We ask ourselves these questions because violent crime is everywhere. Rural. Urban. Male. Female. Young. Old. All races. All ethnic groups. All religions. Anyone can be a victim. No one is exempt and no one is safe. **Violence in America has become a national public health problem of epidemic proportion.**

This book is written to help us better understand the current crisis in violence and what we can do to contain and curtail it. We will examine the latest findings in medicine and the behavioral sciences to help us answer the questions that we have raised in order that we can make some sense of this apparent chaos. In part 1, we examine the risk factors in culture, biology, sociology, and psychology that are thought to contribute to crime. In part 2, we shall use this information to outline specific coping strategies that can be employed by individuals, families, and communities to reduce the risk of violence.

Toward these ends, this first chapter provides us with an overview of America's current culture of violence. We begin by examining the nature and extent of violence in America during the past thirty-five years. Then, we shall review the emergence of the postindustrial state, the cultural context that has been evolving during this same thirty-five-year period. Finally, we look at the impact of the postindustrial state on the basic societal institutions of business, government, the family, school, and religion to see if there are cultural risk factors that may suggest links between the emergence of the postindustrial state and the sharp increases in crime that we are about to review.

Although this topic is difficult, the message of this book is one of hope. We are not helpless in the face of violence. We can reduce this needless human suffering. In this spirit, let us begin our inquiry into the nature of violence.

## The Nature of Violence in America

### *Crimes and Criminals: An Overview*

Since there are many apparent causes of violent crime, it should not surprise us that there are many differing technical definitions, methods of measurement, and systems for recording incidents, and we will consider these viewpoints in subsequent chapters, but we need clear, basic, general definitions to guide us. We shall define violence as the intentional use of physical force to injure or abuse another, and crime as the commission of an act forbidden by public law. Not all violence is criminal (e.g., self-defense) and not all crime is violent (e.g., fraud and embezzlement), but commonly they overlap (e.g., armed robbery). With these basic definitions let us begin to examine the present nature of violent crime in our country.

*Types of Assailants.* There has been enough research over the years to identify basic groupings of assailants, and these are noted in Table 1. Some assailants are ordinary citizens. Overcome with anger, fear, jealousy, and greed, they usually commit crimes on impulse (actions without thought) and are truly sorry for these acts within a short period of time. Most never commit a second crime,

TABLE 1

**Types of Criminals:**

---

Average Citizens
Medically Ill Persons
Domestic Batterers
Disgruntled Employees
Juvenile Delinquents
Career Criminals

---

and the courts deal with these matters in the form of a lesser fine and probation. Medically ill people form the second type of potential assailants. These are persons with disorders such as serious mental illness or pathological intoxication that may lead them to violent outbursts. Depending on the circumstances, these persons may not be held accountable for their crimes. Domestic batterers form a third group. Batterers are usually entitled males who have a past history of being victimized by others, who have a current substance abuse problem, and who feel entitled to treat their spouses and children as their personal property. Disgruntled employees form the next grouping. These are often socially isolated persons with problems of substance abuse and access to weapons. Their jobs mean everything to them so that the threat of job loss provokes violence in some.

The last two categories of assailants are juvenile delinquents and career criminals. These two groups contain many repeat offenders and are responsible for the majority of criminal offenses.

Delinquents are young antisocial individuals. They are aggressive with people and with animals, and are often physically cruel to both. They may destroy property, set fires, and steal the belongings of others. They often stay out late at night and are truant from school.

Without intervention to curtail this antisocial lifestyle, they often mature into career criminals. The failure to conform to social norms continues. Aggressive and deceitful behavior continues, and they learn the skills necessary to commit the most heinous of acts. They continue to repeat these acts over many years because of the thrill of the chase, the monetary rewards, and increases in power and enhanced self-esteem among their criminal peers.

Since delinquents and career criminals are frequently incarcerated, there have been continuous opportunities to study various aspects of their lives. From 1917 to 1976, students of criminology have conducted ten major studies. Two were of adult criminals by psychiatrist Dr. Sheldon Glueck and his wife Eleanor, a social worker. One study assessed male criminals (1939) and the other, female assailants (1934). There were also eight major studies of juvenile delinquents and these are listed in Table 2, on the following page. (The references for all of these scientific studies are included in Appendix A for the interested reader.)

These ten studies provide us with an offender sample of 10,800 persons. Included are both genders, all races, all creeds, all ethnic groups, and representatives from a variety of geographical locations in our country. These studies span a fifty-year period, and the findings are remarkably consistent, an important scientific outcome in its own right.

These offenders came from *broken homes* marred by untimely death, divorce, desertion, separation, foster home placement, and unhappy marriages. *Disrupted family lives* were common and included constant family quarreling, domestic abuse of parents and children, alcoholism, gambling, and profound social isolation. *Inadequate parenting* was the norm with inadequate limit setting by adults, erratic punishment, little parental affection, and general emotional neglect. *Inadequate schooling* was also common with fundamental scholastic and behavioral problems and feelings of academic inferiority.

These characteristics represent many of the biological, sociological, and psychological risk factors that we are to consider, but for our purposes in this chapter, these findings also represent a breakdown in community. The network of stable family life, consistent schooling, and supportive services from other adults in the community was not a part of the lives of these offenders, and it is reasonable to assume that this absence of community may have contributed, at least in part, to their violent lifestyle. We shall return to this theme later in the chapter.

TABLE 2

## Studies of Juvenile Delinquents:

| Study | Number of Subjects | Gender | Major Years of Study | Geographical Location |
|---|---|---|---|---|
| S. and E. Glueck (1940) | 1000 | M | 1920s | MA |
| S. and E. Glueck (1950) | 499 | M | 1940s | MA |
| McCord, McCord, and Zola (1959) | 650 | M | 1940s | MA |
| Konopk (1966) | 181 | F | 1950s | MN |
| Robins (1966) | 524 | M/F | 1950s | MO |
| Wolfgang, Figlio, and Selin (1972) | 3481 | M | 1950s | PA |
| Ahlstrom and Havighurst (1971) | 400 | M | 1960s | MO |
| Tracy, Wolfgang, and Figlio (1990) | 4315 | M | 1970s | PA |

*Types of Violence and Their Measurement.* The types of crimes committed by these assailants are presented in Table 3 and represent the major types of offenses reported in the Federal Bureau of Investigation's (FBI) Uniform Crime Report (UCR). These crimes are known to all of us. Type I offenses are usually the most serious in terms of human suffering, medical expense, sick leave and disability claims, and lost productivity. Type II offenses are the remaining serious categories of criminal

TABLE 3

**FBI Uniform Crime Report: Types of Offenses:**

---

**Type I Offenses:**

Criminal Homicide
Forcible Rape
Robbery
Aggravated Assault
Burglary
Larceny
Auto Theft
Arson

**Type II Offenses:**

Other Assaults
Forgery and Counterfeiting
Fraud
Embezzlement
Stolen Property (buying, receiving, possession)
Vandalism
Weapons (carrying, possession)
Prostitution and Commercialized Vice
Sex Offenses (other)
Narcotic Drug Violation
Gambling
Offenses against Family and Children
Driving under the Influence
Liquor Law Violations
Drunkenness
Vagrancy
All Other Types of Offenses

---

acts that people continually inflict on each other. As you can see from the types of crimes listed, as a country we are clearly having problems living together as a community.

Crime is basically measured in two ways. The first is the FBI UCR, which counts crime reported by individuals and businesses. It counts every separate crime it is informed of and is more accurate for the major crimes or Type I offenses. The second common database is the Bureau of the Census' National Crime Victimization Survey (NCVS). The NCVS counts only personal and household victimizations and relies on the victim's memory, but is generally more accurate for the lesser or Type II offenses. These surveys exclude fraud, drug, white-collar, and victimless crimes.

Obtaining an accurate report of these various offenses, however, is not without its difficulties. In addition to the two differing databases, there are other measurement issues. Some victims do not realize that they are victims and do not report the crime: for example, victims of date rape on campus. Some feel that reporting a crime will be of little use in seeking redress. Still others fear revenge if they should report the assailant. All of these issues are compounded by the fact that, while some police reporting may be somewhat improved, systems vary widely across the country, and there is no way to be sure that the same crimes are being reported with the same accuracy across the country. Even with these limitations, however, the data do reveal clear and dismaying trends that call for our attention.

## The Extent of Violence in America

The extent of violence in our country is frightening. Although we may be more violent than other nations in general, the level of violence within the country is not a constant. Some periods are worse than others, and our own era is one of those high-risk periods. In 1993, 24,526 murders were committed in the United States. That represents sixty-five murders a day. In addition, there were 18,000 assaults per day, with 6,000 of these assaults causing physical injuries.

Although these figures seem straightforward, we are frequently presented with conflicting information about crime. The government reports that it is declining somewhat, yet the media report crimes that seem increasingly aggressive. Which is accurate? Since crime levels fluctuate, we need a clear analysis of these major trends in crime to make sense of these conflicting reports and to fully understand what is happening to us at the present time. Toward that end, Table 4 presents a comparison of the major crime levels in 1960 with those in 1992 from national data compiled by statistician Adam Dobrin and his colleagues (1996). These data present several important findings. Unlike our own day, the period of the early 1960s was generally a low-crime period and serves as a helpful reference point for comparison with the current high levels of violent crime.

As can be seen in Table 4, the first important finding from the statistics is a staggering increase in all levels of violent crime, even after including for better reporting and an increase in the population. The murder rate has doubled. Rape and robbery have increased fivefold, and aggravated assault has increased sixfold. Although victims sometimes know their assailants, increasingly these crimes are being committed by strangers. Thus, the recent declines in violence reported by the government do not necessarily make us feel more safe, because of the enormous increase in crime levels since the 1960s.

## TABLE 4

**Comparative Crime Rates: 1960 and 1992:**

| Type of Crime | Victims* 1960 | 1992 | Age of Assailant | Gender of Assailant | Predominant Race of Assailant |
|---|---|---|---|---|---|
| Homicide | 5.2 | 10.2 | 15-44 | Male | Nonwhite |
| Rape | 8.7 | 42.8 | 15-29 | Male | Nonwhite |
| Robbery | 49.6 | 263.6 | 15-29 | Male | Nonwhite |
| Aggravated Assault | 72.6 | 441.8 | 15-34 | Male | Nonwhite |

* Rates per 100,000

The second finding to emerge from the data is information about the age and gender of the assailants. Here the findings mask two important and opposite trends. One trend is a modest decline in the number of crimes committed by white and nonwhite adult criminals over the age of twenty-four. The second trend is more ominous because it reflects sharp increases in crime by youth (ages fifteen to twenty-four).

For example, the number of young murderers has tripled in the last ten years to 26,000 in 1994, and the number of juvenile murderers using guns during the same period has quadrupled. While most of this violent crime was committed by young males, these statistics also reveal an increase in violent crimes by young girls. Although about thirteen percent of all youth crime is committed by girls, from 1983 to 1992 there was a twenty-five percent increase in violent crimes by young girls, a rate of increase twice as high as that for young males during this same period. These statistics also point to an increase in youthful black assailants, which in some cases may be as great as three to five times that of white-youth assailants.

These statistics on increased youth violence are ominous and worthy of consideration because there are currently thirty-nine million young people under age ten who will shortly enter their teen years, and these teenage years are typically the high-crime years for each generation. The government recently reported the first small decline of 2.9 percent in youth violence for 1995. If this continues, it is an encouraging sign. But far too much remains to be done.

A third finding from these statistics is also masked, and it is that the victims of violence in America are increasingly America's young. Juvenile crime tends to occur after school hours, especially around 3:00 P.M., and often the victims are innocent youth. The National Center for Health Statistics reported that in 1993 more preschoolers were killed by guns than were police officers and United States soldiers shot in the line of duty. The Center also reported that the number of all children dying from gunfire increased ninety-four percent from 1983 (2,951 victims) to 1993 (5,751 victims).

The final finding from the data in Table 4 is the financial cost to society. Addressing crime requires about 550,000 police in 19,691 federal, state, and local policing agents as well as private security agencies with one and a half million employees. A recent Justice Department survey estimated that crime costs our national economy $450 billion each year with an additional $40 billion for prisons and corrections costs.

In reviewing the findings in Table 4, it is clear that we do not feel safe because we are *not* safe, in our communities, our worksites, or our homes.

## The Emergence of the Postindustrial State

How are we to make sense of these sharp increments in all types of violent crime? This is a complex question, but a helpful first step may be to examine the culture in which these changes took place to see whether there are ways to understand why these events may have increased. In fact, a profound social change took place in the culture during this time period as the United States moved from the industrial state to the postindustrial state, and we begin our inquiry there.

## The Industrial State

For much of recorded human history, the human family were small farmers who worked the land, raised animals, and retained a rural lifestyle. This agricultural society underwent a dramatic change in the 1850s. During this period, which continued to the 1970s, energy was harnessed to machines, factories were built, and urban settings began to increase as laborers left the farms for the factories.

This period is known as the Industrial Revolution, and was greatly influenced by science, our understanding of the laws of nature and technology, and the application of those laws to the problems of everyday life. This revolution began when water was harnessed to run spinning looms. It began in Britain and was transported to our own country to Lowell, Massachusetts. In short order, other sources of energy such as steam, coal, oil, electricity, thermal energy, and nuclear energy were similarly harnessed to various types of machines with sharp increases in the amount and variety of material goods, and the country became a dominant world power based on its economic strength.

Great advances in science led to improvements in medicine, sanitation, public health, nutrition, housing, transportation, and communication. A strong economy led to adequate employment, the adequate distribution of goods and services, and an improved quality of life for large numbers of the human family. It was not a perfect system, and there were lean economic years as well as periods of war, but the industrial period created an age of affluence previously unknown in human history. Then in the 1970s, a second major transformation began, and the industrial period itself was uprooted.

## The Postindustrial State

This new transformation has emerged in part from the advent of personal computers. With large numbers of the workforce having access to these machines, the thrust of economic activity in the country shifted from manufactured goods to a knowledge-based society which empha-sizes thinking, research, and discovery. Instead of manufacturing prod-ucts like automobiles and television sets, the new workforce concen-trates on biotechnology, microelectronics, and health care.

This information explosion was accompanied by a second major event, the development of a global economy. In the global economy, companies of all nations compete to sell their goods and services and compete with companies' workers from any corner of the earth to produce the best quality products in the most cost-effective method. We have seen the impact of this new world order in our country in the form of downsizing, layoffs, and mergers as companies adjust to this internationally competitive environment.

These shifts to an information-based society in a global com-petitive marketplace have resulted in a three-tiered stratification of our workforce. The first tier comprises the knowledge workers. These are the men and women who are engaged in scientific research and discovery in the sciences, and who explore the role of com-puter technology for health care, education, and the like, as well as the government leaders at the level of policy development who think out how to put the emerging information to best use for our society as a whole.

The second tier includes those workers who provide services to the knowledge workers. Some of these services are personal, such as those of auto mechanics, hairdressers, and retail store clerks. Others are more directly related to the research and discovery itself, work-ing in banking, finances, real estate, and insurance as well as trans-portation, communications, and utilities.

The third tier is known as the permanent underclass and includes all of those workers who do not have the skills to belong to one of the first two groups. Without the necessary schooling or training to compete for entrance into the first two tiers, members of the permanent underclass have little hope for future advancement and an improved quality of life for themselves and for their children.

The postindustrial state, this knowledge-based society, is having important impacts on the way we live. Individuals have become more mobile in pursuit of employment; many families now have two wage-earning parents, which necessitates child-care; entire neigh-borhoods or communities rise and fall in part dependent on whether they have the resources and workforce needed for the postindustri-al state. We are in a period of major social upheaval, and will remain so for the foreseeable future. [These shifts have been examined in detail by Drucker (1994), Gordon (1996), and Thurow (1996).]

### Values of the Postindustrial State

The industrial state was guided by at least two moral directives from the 1850s to the 1960s: religion as expressed through the Protestant Work Ethic, and the American cultural tradition as expressed in the Declaration of Independence.

In Calvinistic theology, morally good people were thought to be predestined by God to be saved, and these good persons were known by their good works. This theological system and the needs of the industrial state were conjoined, as individuals worked hard to demonstrate their good works, and the economy grew. The Protestant work ethic lent itself to the values of hard work, honesty, self-denial, methodical self-control, sexual exclusivity, and concern for the welfare of one's family and one's neighbors.

The industrial state also drew on the strengths of the Declaration of Independence, which stated that the laws of nature and nature's God were the country's roots, and that each citizen was created with equal inalienable rights to life, liberty, and the pursuit of happiness. These rights were secured by the consent of the governed.

While many still guide their lives by these principles, a radically different set of values is emerging for today's age. Shaped perhaps by natural abundance, instant communication, and freedom of choice, the newer values include a sense of personal entitlement, a focus on material acquisition, and instant gratification of sensate experience.

The sense of personal entitlement emphasizes the importance of the self and its needs with no corresponding sense of responsibility to others or to society at large. Here individuals put their own needs and interests first. While they may allow that they must respect the rights of others, in practice this guideline is soon forgotten or overlooked. The sense of personal entitlement has no moral force other than itself, no transcendent moral authority, and frequently no respect for contractual obligations. Such a view of the self can easily evolve into greed and narcissism with a common outcome of the self versus society.

The focus on material acquisition emphasizes the accumulation of goods and services in their own right, and as a culture we do accumulate. We fill our houses, then fill the attics, then fill the cellars, and then rent extra storage space. We accumulate so many material goods that it is not uncommon for us to have to "enjoy" several of them at once. For example, we turn on the television as we start the microwave for the frozen dinner and talk on the phone as we peruse a current magazine or newspaper. Whereas in an earlier age, material goods might have been used to enhance human interaction (e.g., the family car that permitted a Sunday gathering of the extended family), the newer technologies tend to isolate people from one another as they listen to their headsets, or sit alone before their computer screens. The end result can be a further isolation of people, one from the other.

The third dominant value is instant gratification of the body and its senses. Self-denial and delay of reward are considered obsolete and have been replaced by an emphasis on doing things immediately, running up extensive credit charges, and getting here or there at a moment's notice. This is coupled with a lifestyle of pleasure that emphasizes unfettered sex, drugs, alcohol, intense music, and highly charged lives in general. While in moderation these pleasures sustain life and add occasional zest, in extremes individuals are reduced to anatomy and physiology, and may experience weariness, fatigue, boredom, and ennui.

### Early Outcomes of the Postindustrial State

Although we are still evolving in the postindustrial era, we are able to assess some preliminary measure of its impact on the economy and on society itself.

With regard to the economy, it is clear that we are making important strides for the country. Advances in health and biotechnology and technological advances in transportation, communications, and improved manufacturing processes will improve our quality of life and strengthen our gross domestic product. The United States is an important player on the economic world stage.

A preliminary examination of the impact of the postindustrial state on the social fabric is less encouraging. The emergence of a permanent underclass is a serious social concern. Larger groups of unemployed persons, without the skills to be productive citizens, benefit no one. In addition, recent studies have reported the following additional distressing findings.

1. *Broken Homes.* There is a sharp increase in the loss of intact homes. Divorce is high; desertion is increasing. Out-of-wedlock teenage pregnancies are escalating. Parents are away due to shifts in

the workforce and the need to travel great distances for employment. Some parents are also away from home because they are incarcerated for violent crimes.

2. *Disrupted Family Life.* Statistics from all quarters continue to document unacceptable levels of drug and alcohol use, credit card debt, adultery, nonpayment of child support, family violence between spouses and against children, inadequate housing for families, increasing poverty, and serious social isolation. Stress and depression often follow.

3. *Inadequate Parenting.* Some surveys report that some inadequate parenting is a function of parents with a sense of personal entitlement, who have no true interest in their own children. More common are parents attempting to master one or two jobs for needed income, to provide adequate day care, and to find quality time for family life. This is not easily done in an era of declining incomes, and often the result is latch key children without adequate supervision, without adequate limit setting, without adequate consistency in punishment when warranted, with few true caring attachments to others, and without the ability to learn empathy for others which comes from such attachments. The end result is often feelings of neglect and of being unloved.

4. *Inadequate Schooling.* As tax receipts have declined, governments have had less monies for local services, and many types of programs, including schooling, have been cut. This is a particularly vulnerable area, for without the necessary education today's young people will never be adequately prepared for the postindustrial state, and will find themselves by default in the permanent underclass. It should not surprise us that schools without permanent teachers, without books and supplies, without computers, without adequate physical structure and so forth cannot adequately prepare students for the world in which they must work and live.

We have seen earlier in the chapter how these four factors were found in the lives of the criminals and delinquents who were studied. Could it be that these four factors which were found in small groups of violent people in earlier times have become so pervasive that they can account for the sharp increases in crime in the past thirty-five years? Could the postindustrial transformation somehow be linked to these increases in violent crime? If this were so, what might be the mechanisms in culture to explain these potential linkages?

## Cultural Factors in Violence

Culture may be defined as the customary beliefs, social forms, and material traits of a people. The culture, through its societal institutions of business, government, families, schools, and religions, teaches its members the social norms about how they are to interact with one another in socially beneficial ways so that they are productive citizens for the general welfare of all. Cooperative behavior, joint planning, self-restraint, patience, and concern for others are taught as a means of insuring group survival. These social norms create caring attachments to others and these attachments are fundamental to good physical and mental health and to an absence of violence. In this way the social norms maintain a sense of community.

Cultures change, however, and, while there are evolutionary theories, conflict and systems theories to explain such changes, the structural-functional theory of Émile Durkheim (trans. 1951) appears the most helpful in understanding the impact of our present postindustrial shift.

Durkheim theorized that, in periods of great social upheaval, social norms lose their regulatory force as the social institutions that are the repository of these beneficial guidelines themselves undergo change. In the absence of these moral guidelines, caring attachments are disrupted and individuals feel adrift and not integrated into their normal social networks. The sense of integrated community becomes lost. Durkheim called this tendency for the social norms to lose their regulatory force *anomie*. He supported his theory by reviewing the social disruptions of various countries at various periods in history, and repeatedly found sharp increases in suicides, mental illness, general distress, and violent crime. The emergence of the postindustrial state is just such a period of major social transformation.

Two criminologists and intellectual disciples of Durkheim, Drs. Steven Messner and Richard Rosenfeld (1994) have advanced anomie theory an additional step beyond Durkheim's general theory of cultural change. In their view, the moral voices that reside in government, the family, schools, and religion have been superseded by business and an attitude that any economic end justifies any means, including violence. While this may be true in some cases, it seems unreasonable to single out business by itself. It is the engine that sustains all of us and that has accomplished much. Since ours is a culture that emphasizes personal entitlement and material gain, it perhaps makes more sense to understand that any of our social institutions may be compromised to some extent by these values of entitlement and material gain.

In any case, how might Durkheim's basic general theory of anomie help us understand the possible links between the emergence of the postindustrial state and the recent surge in crime?

First is the act of transformation itself. The social norms and guidelines of the early 1960s were disrupted and their regulatory force weakened. All of our societal institutions were and are in the process of adapting to the new world order. Caring attachments become disrupted and the sense of community is weakened.

Second is the emergence of the permanent underclass, which divides society into the haves and have-nots. The have-nots need to support themselves and their families. If the traditional opportunities for advancement are blocked, some may be forced to criminal acts to survive. Drug dealing as a business venture is one example. Again, the sense of community is weakened.

Third, the values of the postindustrial state themselves further contribute to the loss of community. Personal entitlement, material acquisition, and immediate sensate gratification do not foster concern for the welfare of others. In the absence of broader social norms from our basic institutions that emphasize responsibilities toward others, the problem of community is further exacerbated.

It appears that the anomic conditions of our basic societal institutions, the emergence of the permanent underclass, and the values inherent in the postindustrial state can help us understand in part the broken homes, disrupted family life, inadequate parenting, and inadequate schooling that are associated with much of the violent crime that we have examined. When the cultural sense of community fails, when caring attachments are disrupted, communication and hope often fail as well, and when communication fails, violence may follow.

In addition, there is a further way in which our understanding of the cultural risk factors of anomic conditions and the accompanying sense of uprootedness may lead some to violence. It would appear that anomic conditions are also likely to increase the probability of the biological, sociological, and psychological risk factors being exacerbated. If the cultural controls that regulate social behavior have been weakened in general, then the other specific risk factors are also deregulated. For example, we shall see in the next chapter on the biological risk factors how hyperreactivity of brain chemistry due to drugs and alcohol results in an increased risk for violence. If the societal rules about substance abuse lose their regulatory force, then we are certain to encounter the increased presence of this biological risk factor for violence. Thus, the cultural risk factor of anomie with its deregulation of social norms can result in violence by itself or in interaction with the other also now-loosened risk factors for crime and violence, which themselves can interact with each other.

In this chapter, we have examined our national culture of violence. We have reviewed the actual levels of crime, the major social transformation of the postindustrial state that occurred during the same time period, and how the cultural risk theory of anomie may help us understand the links between the two. We have also seen how anomie with its cultural deregulation also exacerbates the biological, sociological, and psychological risk factors that we will examine in subsequent chapters.

As grim and depressing as this may seem, however, our own history holds an important lesson for us. During the 1880s and 1890s, there was a similar upheaval in our country with attendant social disruption and violence. Durkheim would probably attribute this to anomie resulting from the Industrial Revolution, a major social transformation that preceded our own. In any case, average law-abiding citizens of this earlier period decided collectively to set limits on unlawful, unacceptable, violent behavior and to improve their quality of lives. So can we. When our understanding of the risk factors for violence and crime is complete, we can design a range of specific strategies to contain and prevent their occurrence.

We know from the present chapter that strengthening the sense of community in a period of rapid social change is important. Let us see what the biological, sociological, and psychological risk factors will suggest about why the assailants that we have discussed commit the crimes that we have listed. We begin with the biological risk factors that may be exacerbated in anomic conditions, and the question that most of us ask about assailants: When they do these things, are they literally out of their minds?

# 2

# WHO IN HIS RIGHT MIND
# WOULD DO SUCH A THING?:
# BIOLOGICAL FACTORS
# IN VIOLENCE

*Is there any cause in nature that makes these hearts hard?*
— William Shakespeare

*Life is "solitary, poor, nasty, brutish and short."*
— Thomas Hobbes

*Dateline: Framingham, Massachusetts. August 28, 1995.*

357•BAN

This was heady stuff. From working-class roots to the fifty-sixth floor of one of the largest insurance companies in the United States. He had risen to become one of only twenty-four senior financial analysts and the only one to represent his company with the state's business and government leaders in the planning of the new sports complex for the city of Boston.

Soft-spoken, slow to anger, and with intense facial features, the analyst was so unlike his wife, whom he had met in the company and who was a wonderful counterbalance in his life. Outgoing and supportive of him, she was full of life, and they were known within the company as a "Mutual Life Insurance couple." Coming from a childhood marked by divorce, his wife was determined to create a truly happy and loving home. Theirs was the American Dream.

357•BAN

There were darker moments, of course. Every life had its problems and sorrows. There were periods of domestic battering. There had been the death of their son in February 1994. Born three-and-one-half months premature, he had died within fourteen hours from cardiopulmonary failure, the medical term for underdeveloped heart and lungs. He and his wife were devastated by this loss, and he had spent long hours in their television room, pondering videotapes of the dead baby's sonograms and fetal monitoring. His sadness lifted with the birth of his daughter Melissa, four-and-a-half months ago, but the couple had learned just this month that little Melissa had an abnormally formed hip. He had recently begun to attend synagogue more regularly.

357•BAN

The intense, slow-to-anger senior analyst followed that license plate on the car ahead of him for several miles. Little Melissa was with him in the back seat of the car. When the driver of the first car reached his own home, the analyst, who had been following him, engaged the first driver in a conversation about .357 magnums and gun control. The police were called and blood stained clothing was found in the analyst's car. He was arrested when he acknowledged having done something terribly wrong.

Police were dispatched to the analyst's home. On the second floor, they found additional bloody clothing and a butcher's knife. In the backyard they found a wooden stake impaled with two lungs and a heart. Thirty yards away, they found the analyst's wife, her face badly bruised, her chest slit open from throat to navel. A softball size rock covered with blood lay nearby in the stillness of the night.

357•BAN

Successful senior financial analyst . . . . A company couple . . . . Insured for life.

Criminologists call this type of a murder one of "overkill," in which the assailant experiences a passionate rage that is driven by an excessive need for power and control. How someone could feel so powerless, how an important corporate executive could feel so helpless that it led to murder is difficult to understand and takes us to the heart of an age-old debate. It is known as the Nature/Nurture argument. In understanding how a human being acts or behaves, is that act primarily biological (Nature) or a function of the person's interaction with the environment (Nurture)?

The Nature proponents believe that we are born with a brain and a nervous system that contain structures and chemicals that permit human beings to think and function as living organisms. These protagonists of Nature also believe biology to be the overriding determining factor in accounting for what human beings do, including violent acts.

The Nurture proponents argue that the social environmental context in which the person functions is the most important factor in determining human behavior. An environment with a range of adequate resources and opportunities results in normal growth and development, and is the more likely cause of adaptive human behavior. Similarly, inadequate resources such as poverty, racism, inadequate schooling, and the like are equally important factors in negative human outcomes.

This is more than an academic question, for its answer very much shapes the types of remedial interventions that are apt to be selected. For example, in our present discussion of violence, if we believe violence to be primarily biological in origin, we are more likely to use the resources of society to develop medicines or surgical interventions to prevent violence from occurring. If, on the other hand, we believe violence to be an expression of the social environment, then our energies might be expended on improving the quality of life with enhanced employment opportunities, better laws for managing drug abuse, and the like.

As with most polarized positions in science, the evidence suggests that both Nature and Nurture are at work. Research on the serious mental illnesses of schizophrenia and manic depression, and research on alcoholism suggest biological determinants in some cases, and social determinants in others, and sometimes an admixture of both. We shall see what the findings have to tell us about the Nature/ Nurture argument and violent crime as we proceed.

The present chapter focuses on a comprehensive review of the possible biological risk factors for violence that may be exacerbated and unleashed during anomic periods when the sense of community is weakened. After a brief discussion of brain structure and functions, we shall review the ethological and genetic studies of violence as well as the extensive research on brain injuries, medical illnesses, and altered brain states that have been associated with aggressive outbursts.

Our inquiry will be formed by the questions raised by the Framingham murder. How would we explain this and other acts of violence? Is it all biologically rooted? We begin with the human nervous system.

## The Human Nervous System

The cortex, limbic system, and the nervous system itself are three aspects of the human nervous system that are thought to be involved in some cases of violence that appear biologically based, at least in part. In the latter component we want to pay particular attention to the information transmission components known as synaptic gaps.

*The Cortex.* The cortex is our thinking brain. It receives all of the information from our senses, scans memory for past similar experiences, evaluates what needs to be done, and then plans and implements the solution to whatever problem we may be encountering. The cortex is involved in social learning, reasoning, moral judgments, and anticipation of the consequences of our behavior. Since these are the very skills which some assailants appear to lack, it is reasonable to assume that damage to the cortex may be associated with some violent acts. Birth defects, head injuries, tumors, viruses, exposure to noxious chemical agents, autoimmune disorders, and vitamin deficiencies have all been known to cause injuries to the cortex and to result in subsequent violent behavior in some cases.

*The Limbic System.* The limbic system is embedded in the center of the brain, underneath the cortex, to protect it from injury. It is small, about the size of a thimble, but it is protected because it has an important role to play in human behavior. It is the limbic system that adds feeling tone to our experience. For example, two people see a fire in the distance. One is frightened, as that person remembers a house being burned to the ground. The other feels relaxed, as that person remembers fires in the hearth during winter. It is the limbic system that is involved in these two different "feeling" outcomes.

The limbic system has many smaller substructures within it. Two of these are the hypothalamus and the amygdala, and it has been shown that, when these components are activated in some people, persistent and negative emotions occur and persist. These negative feelings can include intense anger and rage. In this way, the limbic system may be involved in some types of violent behaviors.

*The Nervous System and Brain Chemistry.* Contrary to the thinking of some, the nervous system is not a few long fibers in the body, but rather a network of many smaller fibers that inervate the body to bring information to the brain through our senses and to direct the body to respond with different courses of action. These nerve fibers are connected by microscopic balloon-like vesicles known as synaptic gaps. These synaptic gaps contain various chemicals, and when these chemicals are present in the correct amounts, the information to or from the brain is transferred smoothly from one nerve fiber to the next. Synaptic gaps act like a drum head and resonate to carry the information clearly from one nerve to the next nerve. When this occurs, the person functions smoothly. When the chemicals are not in their proper balance, the person does not function efficiently and may become oversensitive or "hyperreactive" to events, even relatively minor events. For example, a bus backfires, and a pedestrian's nerves are frayed to the point of anger. Hyperreactivity is physiological irritability and may result in angry and violent outbursts.

Many different bodily states can cause hyperreactivity. These may include pain, hunger, lack of sleep, hypoglycemia (low blood sugar), excessive heat and humidity, overcrowding, and general life stress, all of which on occasion have been associated with violent outbursts. Similarly, drug and alcohol abuse may alter normal brain chemistry and cause hyperreactivity and subsequent violence.

There are at least five chemicals within the body itself that are thought to be associated with violence. Three are neurotransmitters in the synaptic gaps (epinephrine, norepinephrine, and serotonin) and two are hormones (testosterone and estrogen).

Under life stress, the adrenal glands emit adrenaline. Adrenaline becomes converted to epinephrine in the body and mobilizes the body to respond quickly by increasing heart rate, breathing, muscle tone, and the like. Similarly, adrenaline becomes converted to norepinephrine in the brain, and rivets it's attention to the problem at hand so that efficient, and possibly life-saving, problem-solving is assured. Epinephrine and norepinephrine have been shown to be present in aggressive outbursts.

The third common chemical in the synaptic gaps is serotonin. It helps to keep individuals calm, relaxed, and generally content. When serotonin is depleted, persons usually become irritable, angry, unhappy, and ultimately depressed. If the depression is profound and/or long-lasting, it may result in violence against others or, more often, violence against the self in the form of suicide.

The remaining body chemicals of interest to us are the sex hormones, testosterone and estrogen. Found in males in the testes and produced in females by the adrenal cortex, testosterone, especially in young males between the ages of fifteen and twenty-four, is thought by some to be responsible for much of the violence in this age group. Overlooked are the pro-social adaptive strengths of testosterone such as increased energy, assertiveness, and sexual arousal, in the belief that testosterone and its association with violence outweighs any benefits that it may have to offer. However, the research evidence is fairly straightforward: there is no clear association between testosterone in and of itself and violent outbursts (Archer, 1994). While it may be a contributing factor in some cases, it is not an overriding factor. Similar is the common belief by many that decreases in estrogen may lead to aggressive behavior, but again the research findings are consistent. There are no clear associative links that estrogen by itself is an overriding biological risk factor.

Although our review to this point suggests a possible link between violence and the nervous system in some cases (such as head injury to the cortex that may result in biologically rooted crime), assessing the role of biology in aggression is usually far more complicated. For example, is the person who drinks excessively, then drives a motor vehicle and kills someone with that car considered to be violent solely due to hyperreactivity of the nervous system? Did the person have a choice not to drink? If the person was already addicted to alcohol, did the person still have a choice?

In most cases, it is fairly difficult to determine whether there are biological risk factors in any given act of aggression, and even more difficult to determine whether biology or Nature was the overriding factor. With this in mind, let us look at the biological roots by reviewing the evidence for ethology, genetics, and medical illness. Let us ask the most fundamental question about violence first: are violent people born this way?

## Biological Roots of Violence

### *Ethology*

We have heard the expressions: "It's a jungle out there." "Cut-throat competition." "Lean and mean." "Kill or be killed." "It's the survival of the fittest." Each of these expressions implies that we humans at times act aggressively to ensure survival, that we do this instinctively, and that we are born with this mechanism to act violently in the right circumstances.

Instincts are usually defined as largely inheritable and unalterable tendencies in organisms, including humans, to make complex and specific responses to various environmental circumstances without involving reasoning. We act impulsively without thinking about it. Are humans who behave aggressively driven by instinct? Do we become angry, violent, and even murderous without thinking about our behavior and its consequences?

A good many scholars have answered this question and, as with other aspects of the Nature/Nurture argument, some answer in the affirmative and some in the negative.

Beginning in the 1960s, ironically, when the crime rates were low, as we have seen, there was remarkable cultural interest in whether humans were born with innate, unmanageable aggression. Perhaps it was the cumulative effect of two world wars, the Holocaust, the Korean Conflict, assassinations of political leaders, and the beginning of the Vietnam War. Many individuals appeared to want a better understanding of the carnage throughout the century. Three books, *The Territorial Imperative* (Ardrey, 1966), *On Aggression* (Lorenz, 1966), and *The Naked Ape* (Morris, 1967) crystallized the national interest in aggression. Might people be born to be violent?

Each of these authors believed that aggression was instinctual, that it occurred automatically, and that this reaction was essentially free of reason. This view of human Nature can be traced back to the English philosopher Thomas Hobbes, who viewed the world as a basic struggle of all persons against each other. This theme was intensified by a Darwinian ideologue named Herbert Spencer, who coined the phrase "the survival of the fittest."

Dr. Charles Darwin (1995 edition) was a physician and zoologist who studied species of plants in the nineteenth century. He proposed the theory of Natural Selection to explain why some species survived and others became extinct. The principles of this process were mutation and selection. Gradually, plants were affected by the environments in which they grew. Subtle changes modified each species of plant to enable it to adapt to the changing environment. These changes produced slight genetic mutations that continued when the plants reproduced themselves. Changes that were adaptive led to continued growth and survival in this natural cycle. Spencer applied the theory to a human's strength to survive. Richard Ardrey, Konrad Lorenz, and Desmond Morris essentially adopted this position.

In his early work, Ardrey proposed that humans were instinctually aggressive because our human ancestors were animals that were carnivorous, predatory, and cannibalistic (Ardrey, 1966). He had refined his theory by 1966 with a focus primarily on what he referred to as the human territorial imperative. Humans were thought to have an innate, instinctual desire to acquire and then defend territory. In Ardrey's reasoning, status was the aggressive pressure to achieve social dominance, and by holding and defending territory, when it was invaded, humans gained social status.

Desmond Morris (1967) expanded on this theme. In Morris's reasoning, humans were instinctually aggressive in three situations. These included fighting to establish territorial rights over a piece of land, to establish dominance in the social order, and to protect one's family. Interspecies aggression was primarily to control others, whereas intraspecies fighting was to subdue others.

Konrad Lorenz (1966) sounded similar themes. Drawing on his work with animals, he reasoned that innate aggression served distinct purposes. First, aggressive behavior insured the spacing of the species uniformly over the habitat to guarantee survival of the greatest number. Second, instinctual aggression was important in mate selection to breed better-qualified creatures. Third, aggression within the species led to the formation of a dominant social order that provided leadership and discipline for the greater good of the group.

These popular writings received apparent support from a book on sociobiology by academic sociobiologist Edmund Wilson (1975). Wilson argued that the same basic reasoning of the biology of genetics could be extended to our understanding of social behavior without any change in assumptions. Dr. Wilson and his colleagues, evolutionary psychologists Martin Daly and Margo Wilson (Archer, 1994), then studied the data relating to various violent acts such as infanticide and spousal murder. Dr. Daly and Wilson found that parents murdered their own offspring if the children were unlikely to reap essential fitness benefits. In another survey of spousal abuse data in North America, they found that men killed women who abandoned them or threatened to do so, as an act of coercive exclusivity or in anger over questions of paternal assurance. All of these findings were taken in support of evolutionary survival.

Such arguments did not go unanswered. Building on the work of philosophers John Locke and Jean Jacques Rousseau, who believed humans to be benevolent in Nature and shaped by the environment rather than by inherited instincts, behavioral scientists Ashley Montagu (1978) and Francis de Waal (1989) pointed to the role of learning in aggression and to the series of checks and balances that held aggression in check. They, too, began their defense within the context of Darwin's work. Instead of focusing on survival as a selfish strategy, they pointed out that Darwin's many examples implied cooperative interaction for successful outcomes.

Dr. Montagu was firm in his view that much of human behavior was learned, not instinctual, and he was prolific in reviewing the evidence for nonaggressive societies around the world. Citing the Arapesh of New Guinea, the Semai of Malaya, and the Hopi of North America, among others, he was able to demonstrate that, at least, smaller human societies were conducted on nonviolent principles in all corners of the earth. In support of this, anthropologists and other behavioral scientists have been able to document other strategies to avoid conflict, including approaches such as avoidance, ignoring, negotiating, mediating, arbitration, and adjudication as evidence that humans can solve problems without being instinctively aggressive (Whiteford and Friedle, 1992).

A similar view of human Nature has been put forth by ethologist Francis de Waal (1989). In studying primate chimpanzees over long periods of time, Dr. de Waal noticed that some forms of aggression did occur in his animal colonies. Often, these encounters are to insure dominance or to keep peace, and they are almost always followed in short order by attempts at reconciliation, often in the form of touching. De Waal concludes from his research that aggression is not instinctual, that it is in part learned, and that there is a system of checks and balances to keep such aggression from becoming destructive of the individual and his family or community.

Perhaps a fitting way to conclude this debate is to examine what we know of cannibalism. Humans eating other humans ought to give us clear evidence of instinctual aggression if such a tendency exists. Anthropologist Dr. Hermann Helmuth (Montagu, 1978) did a worldwide survey of what is known about why humans eat other humans, and found that in the distant past, when this practice occurred, it was often motivated by the wish to remain with the dead, to attain their strength and power as well as for mockery or to prevent revenge. These acts were based on myths, beliefs, and rituals, and were only occasionally signs of impulsive rage.

Where does all of this evidence about instincts lead us? The preponderance of the evidence argues against the presence of overriding aggressive instincts in humans, except in situations of self-defense in the face of immanent harm. Humans do have the capacity to act in anger and rage toward others, but we are not born to do this. There is a system of checks and balances both within the individual and within the social environment to modify these conflicts in adaptive, cooperative ways. If the social environment is weakened and without norms, aggression may increase, but it does not appear to be innate.

## Genetics

Since there is no clear evidence that humans are born with an instinct to act aggressively toward others, the next step is to see if there is any other biological evidence that violence, aggression, and criminal behavior may be genetically determined.

There have been several reports of intergenerational violence in which both the parents and their children behave in antisocial and criminal ways. The problem with these findings is that we have no way of knowing whether it is the family genetic structure or the family environment that is causing these aggressive outcomes.

In large measure, medicine and the behavioral sciences have sought to answer these Nature/Nurture questions through what are known as twin studies. On the assumption that the biological component must be similar within families, some twin studies compare monozygotic twins from the same egg with dizygotic fraternal twins from two different eggs. If the measured trait is higher in monozygotic than fraternal twins, genetics is thought to be important.

A more refined approach to twin studies is to employ twins adopted and reared apart from birth as a better way to separate possible biological or Nature effects from environmental factors. Because of the complexity of biology and the rich diversity of everyday experience, such research is not easily conducted.

The basic approach is to hold the biological factors constant in two or more differing environments. If there are substantially different behavioral outcomes, then the outcome is probably due to environmental factors since the biological or genetic factor is constant. However, if the outcome is essentially the same in the differing environments, then biological factors are considered the more likely explanation since the differing environment would not appear to be exerting undue influence on the end result.

In medicine, investigators usually try to use identical monozygotic twins so that they know that the biology of each twin is the same. In addition, they study only those monozygotic twins who have been truly reared apart since birth, as might occur in case of immediate adoption or of the mother's death or serious illness. Next, the researchers are careful to include only those pairs of monozygotic twins who had been reared in home environments that were highly similar. For example, one pair of twins might have been adopted by two urban upper-middle-class families. A second set of twins may have been placed in rural middle-class farm families. Attention is paid to the family income level, number of stepsiblings, level of educational opportunity, recreational possibilities, and the like. With this level of research precision, the impact of possible biological or genetic influences can be separated from possible environmental factors. If the crime rate is similar, it is most likely due to Nurture. If the rates differ, Nature is more likely implicated.

## What Have the Studies Found?

Preliminary surveys of families and twins suggested higher rates of criminal behavior in some families than in others. These studies were small in size and lacked the experimental rigor that we have just outlined but, taken as a whole, these studies suggested the possibility of genetic influences. The search was begun.

In 1965, a specific genetic theory was proposed. It was suggested by some researchers that some men with an extra Y chromosome were more aggressive than men with the normal XY configuration. Known as the XYY theory, it was ultimately disproved. However, research methods were improving, and the types of more refined twin studies that we have noted were being conducted.

Science writer Angela Turner has provided the most recent and complete review of this body of scientific data (Archer, 1994). In the various studies that examined aggression itself in adults, there was little evidence of a genetic basis in the face of many conflicting results. Part of the confusion stems from poor definitions of aggression in each study and from the use of surveys and crime statistics to measure aggression. Studies of aggression in young children again provided no clear outcomes. Rough-and-tumble behavior in children is normal, and it is not always easy to infer that such behavior is motivated primarily by aggressive feelings.

Adoption studies that have measured antisocial behavior in adults offer some suggestion of a genetic predisposition toward criminal behavior. However, studies of juvenile delinquents of monozygotic twins and of fraternal twins reared together suggest more environmental factors, such as one twin influencing the other through peer pressure.

Studies of adult criminality yield somewhat more substantial evidence of a genetic predisposition both in studies of identical and fraternal twins reared together as well as in adoption studies. For example, in one adoption study, the adoptees of criminal biological mothers were more likely to commit crimes. This relationship between criminal behaviors in both adoptees and biological parents appears to be true in the case of habitual offenders.

In summary, there is no true consistent evidence for a genetic basis for aggression, antisocial behavior, delinquency, or criminality. In fact, at least for human aggressive behavior, these studies provide substantial evidence for the importance of environmental factors such as parental attitudes, parental discipline, and adult role models, the same general findings reported in chapter 1.

However, twin studies of personality traits other than crime itself provide some evidence (as much as forty to fifty percent in some cases) that some components of personality may predispose some individuals to react in anger, display antisocial behavior, or even engage in criminal acts in some contexts. Factors such as sociability, emotionality, and one's basic activity level appear to have some inheritable component. Low intelligence, impulsiveness, hyperactivity, sensation-seeking, and neuroticism or constant worrying about details are some of those that have been identified. These factors are not genetically linked to violent crime in themselves, but predispose some individuals with these traits to react in antisocial ways. For example, a person with low intelligence who is easily frustrated (emotionality) might strike out at someone, if the person's needs were not being immediately met. The research evidence that suggests that some personality traits may predispose to subsequent aggression and antisocial behavior is extensive, well designed, and consistent in its findings.

Since the 1980s, research methods for studying genetics have been improved even more, and now permit examination of the genetic deoxyribonucleic acid (DNA) itself. By using large sample sizes of twins reared together and apart and employing more powerful tools for statistical analysis, the ability to understand possible genetic components has greatly increased. Most recent findings suggest that there is no simple answer to the question of a genetic basis for violent and aggressive behavior. The most recent DNA research suggests that, whereas one gene may lead to violence in one person, that similar gene in another may not. The genetic expression of violence appears to be more complex and most probably involves multiple genes in linear and nonlinear interactions (Bouchard, 1994). If there is a genetic basis for aggression, its Nature remains unknown.

## TABLE 1

**Medical Conditions in Human Violence:**

| Medical Disorder | Age of Onset |
|---|---|
| Mental Retardation | Birth |
| Attention Deficit/ Hyperactivity Disorder | Birth |
| Serious Mental Illness | Late Teens Onward |
| Intermittent Explosive Disorder | Twenties or Thirties |
| Organic Personality Syndrome | Usually under Thirty/ over Fifty |
| Temporal Lobe Epilepsy | Any Age |
| Post-Traumatic Stress Disorder | Any Age |
| Alcohol/Drug Abuse | Any Age |
| Depression/Suicide | Any Age |
| Dementia | Usually over Fifty |
| *Personality Disorders* | *Age of Onset* |
| Conduct Disorder | Before Age Fifteen |
| Antisocial Personality Disorder | After Age Fifteen |
| Borderline Personality Disorder | Usually Twenties |
| Paranoid Personality Disorder | Any Age |

## Medical Illnesses

We turn our attention next to exploring the various ways in which biological illnesses may result in violent crime. This is probably the way most of us explain to ourselves the otherwise inexplicable horror of violence. We assume the person was medically ill or insane, and surely not in his or her right mind when the act was committed. How could someone freely choose to commit these heinous acts? Surely, the brains of these cruel and inhumane persons cannot be normal. In this section, we want to examine the various medical disorders that can result in violent and aggressive behavior, medical conditions in which the violence has clear biological risk determinants. However, this is only half of our task, for, once we have established the medical basis of an individual act of violence, we still need to ask whether the act was fully biological and fully beyond the control of the violent offender.

### Medical Conditions

We begin with the basic medical conditions and four personality disorders that are listed in Table 1. All have been associated with violence against the self or others. Our inquiry begins with the disorders present at birth and during childhood.

1. *Mental Retardation.* Mental retardation is seriously limited intellectual functioning. While none of us is necessarily good at every intellectual task, in general our level of skills for reading, comprehension, spelling, and reasoning is adequate enough to permit us to lead normal lives and to solve most of the daily problems we encounter. Mental retardation is marked by very limited skills in *all* areas of intellectual functioning. This includes social, academic, sensori-motor, vocational, self-help, and communication skills. It limits the individual's ability to respond and these limitations may result in violent and aggressive outbursts in some instances.

There are many causes for mental retardation, and some of the more common ones include genetic abnormalities such as Down's Syndrome or phenylketonuria; accidents; environmental hazards such as mercury or lead poisoning; and noxious chemicals. In this last category, Fetal Alcohol Syndrome (FAS) is increasingly observed. FAS arises from the heavy use of alcohol by the mother during the pregnancy. It can retard the growth of the fetus and cause low birth weight; small stature;

cranial, facial, and limb abnormalities; and mental retardation. Finally, some mental retardation is due to cultural deprivation where the child's brain is not stimulated and intellectual functioning does not mature. In other cases, there is no known cause.

2. *Attention Deficit/Hyperactivity Disorder (ADHD)*. ADHD is another birth disorder that is associated with violence. Children with this disorder are characterized by excessive energy and activity. They may be disorganized, tactless, obstinate, bossy, always on the go, inattentive, and impulsive. They have generally poor academic and social skills, and their youthful misconduct may lead to violence toward others in their childhood and adolescent years.

Like mental retardation, a number of theories have been advanced to explain this behavior. Genetics is one. Biochemical theories, such as allergies to food additives, form a second theory, and psychological theories form another category. An example of this latter type of theoretical explanation is that of the child with a predisposition to be overactive and moody, whose mother is impatient and easily stressed. The parent-child battleground that ensues is offered as an explanation of subsequent hyperactivity in some children.

3. *Serious Mental Illness*. The serious mental illnesses are medical diseases and include schizophrenia, manic-depressive, and recurring major depressive episodes. Although a major depressive episode can happen to anyone in the face of severe loss, in some individuals they recur at regular intervals. Schizophrenia, manic-depressive illness, and recurring depressive episodes are medical problems that run in families, that often begin in adolescence, and that flare up from time to time just as the medical problems of diabetes and arthritis often have flare ups. There are medicines to control these illnesses effectively.

However, without the medicines, there are changes in brain chemistry called *psychosis*, which may lead to false beliefs and delusions (e.g., "the aliens want my bicycle") in altered sensory experiences (e.g., hearing voices of people who are not there), and in altered thinking patterns. The voices are often persecutory in Nature and may command the patient to harm himself or herself or someone else for protection. This risk is particularly high if the mentally ill person who is hearing persecutory voices has also been drinking. The disinhibition of the cortex by the alcohol, coupled with the altered sensory experience, produces the highest risk in serious mental illness for violent behavior of some kind.

*4. Intermittent Explosive Disorder.* A second disorder that begins in young adulthood is intermittent explosive disorder. Persons with this medical condition are characterized by sudden, unexpected outbursts of aggression that bear no real relation to the events that are occurring. These men and women are not intoxicated, do not have serious mental illness, and are not psychopaths. When the episode has passed, they are greatly chagrined and embarrassed, and apologize immediately. The reasons for this behavior remain unknown, but some medical scientists speculate that this may be some form of limbic system dysfunction.

*5. Organic Personality Syndrome.* This medical syndrome usually occurs in persons under thirty or over fifty years of age and is directly related to brain injury. These injuries may include brain tumors, viral infections such as encephalitis or rabies, cerebral vascular accidents and strokes, multiple sclerosis, Huntington's chorea, some forms of mental retardation, accidents involving head injury, and prolonged substance abuse. These biological traumas often result in sudden violent behavior for which there may be no real precipitant in the environment.

*6. Temporal Lobe Epilepsy.* The temporal lobe is the part of the brain that is involved in processing, storing, and retrieving memories. Disruptions in brain functioning in these nerve fibers will result in seizures. Epilepsy primarily affects children and young adults but it can occur at any age. In about seventy percent of the cases, there is no known cause. In the remaining cases, evidence may be found for maternal influences during pregnancy, head trauma from accidents and gunshot wounds, brain tumors, infections, or poisonings such as that induced by excessive use of alcohol. While most persons with epilepsy are not violent, seizure behavior in some may at times be associated with aggressive outbursts toward others.

*7. Post-Traumatic Stress Disorder (PTSD).* The violence toward others that we are studying in this book can ironically cause those victims to themselves become violent at a later time.

Psychological trauma is the person's response to a sudden, unexpected, potentially life-threatening event over which the person has no control, no matter what that person tries to do (Flannery, 1992, 1994). The neurotransmitters epinephrine and norepinephrine, which we discussed earlier, flood the body and mind of the victim, immediately mobilize the victim physiologically for the emergency situation at hand, and may result in temporary hyperreactivity.

Victims may have common symptoms that may include hypervigilance, sleep disturbances, exaggerated startle response, and intrusive recollections of the event.

If the traumatic event is sustained, the presence of norepinephrine may sensitize the limbic system and lead to permanent hyperreactivity in the face of subsequent life stress, which at times may result in aggressive outbursts. This process of limbic sensitization is called *kindling*. Untreated psychological trauma becomes PTSD after a few months have passed.

Recent research on both violent adults and juvenile delinquents have shown some in both groups to have past personal histories of being victims themselves, and this past history of personal violence in some cases appears implicated in violent acts that they commit against others at a later date. At the very least, untreated PTSD may result in a low-grade depressive state until death.

8. *Alcohol/Drug Abuse.* Alcohol and drugs are substances that alter brain chemistry and disinhibit the cortical control centers in the brain that prevent violence, so it should not be surprising that the use and abuse of those substances may result in violent acts. Alcohol, amphetamines, barbiturates, crack/cocaine, and PCP are all known to be related to violence toward others.

People abusing drugs generally tend to prefer the use of one drug over others. Psychiatrist Edward Khantzian (1985) has a theory to explain this pattern of preference in substance abuses. He believes that these men and women are using the drugs to self-medicate painful feeling states. This self-medication hypothesis, for which Khantzian has research evidence, suggests that substance abusers who use barbiturates and alcohol are treating anxiety. Those who are primarily using amphetamines or crack/cocaine are treating depression, and that those who use opiates are medicating intense anger and rage. It may well be that some current substance abuse is an attempt to self-medicate the dysphoric states that accompany our present levels of anomie.

In any case, in persons who are abusing substances, the aggressive outbursts can be prompted by the individual's personal problems exacerbated by the drugs, because of the direct action of the drugs on brain chemistry itself, by side effects caused by the combination of several different types of drugs in the brain at the same time, or because of withdrawal effects as the drugs are secreted from the body.

In addition, some individuals have a medical condition known as *pathological intoxication*. These individuals are unable to consume alcohol in any amount, including trace amounts, without becoming violent. It is unclear why this happens, but it is clear that aggression will likely follow any ingestion of this drug.

9. *Depression/Suicide.* Serious clinical depression is marked by loss of physical energy and loss of psychological interest in one's daily activities and goals. Feelings of sadness, anger, guilt, and hopelessness may be accompanied by loss of appetite, irregular sleep patterns, problems concentrating and remembering, and bouts of tears. Interest in sexual activity wanes or is absent. It is as if the person has come to a slow, grinding halt.

If the depressive state is severe enough, the individual may develop a depressed psychotic state with false beliefs. Sometimes, these beliefs are persecutory in Nature (e.g., "the neighbors are running their lawn mowers to harm my cat's hearing") or false beliefs about the self (e.g., "worms are eating my intestines"). In cases such as these, especially with persecutory delusions present, the depressed individual may become violent toward others.

Serious depression may also lead to violence against the self in the form of suicide. There are two forms of suicidal behavior to consider. The first is people who gesture so that others will not leave them. A young woman takes too many sleeping pills but "arranges" to be found, and knows that her ex-boyfriend will return in guilt and fear. Gestures are usually superficial, although the individual always runs the risk of accidental death.

The second category of suicides is found in those depressed individuals who intentionally take their own lives by lethal doses of poisons, gunshots, stabbings, drownings, or running in front of oncoming vehicles. These people want to die, plan to die, and implement their plans. The pain associated with life is too intense to endure any longer. Paradoxically, when the plans for death are in place, some individuals become more relaxed and peaceful as they await their deaths.

Medical evidence from Scandinavia (Justice, 1988) suggests that some depressed individuals who commit suicide may have abnormally low levels of serotonin in their bodies and have a lower threshold for life's stressful situations. It is unknown whether serotonin burns abnormally fast in these persons or whether they are born this way. Research is now ongoing to answer these questions.

10. *Dementia.* Dementia is marked by serious deficits in brain cognitive capacities and can include problems with memory, language, motor skills, and executive problem-solving. Dementia can

occur for many reasons; some of the more common are Alzheimer's Disease, Parkinson's Disease, Huntington's Disease, brain tumors, cerebrovascular accidents, vitamin deficiencies, neurosyphilis, and substance abuse.

Some demented people may become aggressive and violent. Assaults on family members or health care staff are common examples. While the reasons for violence vary by individual, common to all is the disinhibition of the cortical control centers in the brain that prevent aggression.

### Personality Disorders

The second grouping of medical problems that we want to examine is personality disorders. While any of us may occasionally have a poor solution to a particular problem, personality disorders reflect ingrained, long-standing faulty patterns of coping with life's problems that result in great distress to others and/or the self. We noted earlier that certain personality traits may predispose some individuals to react aggressively in some circumstances and that these traits are sometimes found in these personality disordered individuals. The disorders most often associated with violence are listed in Table 1 and are reviewed here.

1. *Conduct Disorders*. While not a personality disorder as such, many conduct-disordered children become antisocial personalities as adults, so it is important for us to understand these early breeding grounds of adult criminal behavior. Conduct disorders are found in children under fifteen years of age and are marked by temper outbursts, mood irritability, poor social skills at home and at school, and poor academic achievement. Some have ADHD, and many have themselves been victims of violence at home or on the streets.

2. *Antisocial Personality Disorder*. These individuals continually disregard society's rules and values, do what they want (often at the expense of others), and have little apparent anxiety or guilt about the consequences of their behavior for themselves. Recent research findings have shown *some* antisocial persons to have abnormal electro-encephalograms (EEGs) or brain-wave readings and a higher evidence of attention disorders.

3. *Borderline Personality Disorder*. Persons with this disorder are impulsive and moody, and they have limited problem-solving skills, especially interpersonal skills. They experience chronic feelings of

loneliness and abandonment, and in the face of intense frustration, anger, or life stress may become aggressive toward others or, more commonly, toward themselves. Delicate cutting of one's own wrists is a common form of self-aggression.

4. *Paranoid Personality Disorder.* This disorder is marked by unwarranted suspicion of others, basic mistrust of the world, hostility, social isolation, and poor problem-solving skills. The expectation of harm at the hands of others frequently results in swift counterattacks. This disorder can occur at any age, and, while it is thought by some to be related to depression, the true cause remains unknown at present.

Let us return now to the two questions that we posed as we began this review of medical conditions: (1) Are there biological risk factors for violence, and (2) Are these biological conditions always beyond the person's control? The answer to the first question is clearly in the affirmative. A review of the conditions noted in Table 1 indicates that each of them has possible biological risk factors.

Are these conditions the sole agent in acts of violence? Here the answer is less clear. In some conditions, such as organic personality syndrome and some forms of dementia, persons are not usually considered responsible for their behavior since the cortical inhibitory centers of the brain have been irreversibly damaged. However, what of the other conditions for which there are effective treatments? In cases of the first episode of the violent outbursts associated with an as yet undiagnosed condition, the individual would not probably be held responsible for the violence. For example, if you did not know that you had pathological intoxication until your first encounter with alcohol, you would not likely be held responsible for your outburst. However, if this condition was diagnosed and you continued to drink, then you would most likely be held responsible for subsequent violence. The same is true for persons with serious mental illness and substance abuse. As a general principle, if there is no overriding cortical damage and the condition has been diagnosed and treated, persons with medical conditions who disregard the treatments for those illnesses are usually held responsible for their behavior, including violent behavior. Similarly, persons with personality disorders are usually held responsible for their behaviors. While there are some personality traits that are associated with aggression and some milder forms of cortical problems, as we have seen, these factors are not severe enough to override one's sense of being held personally accountable for one's acts.

As we conclude our review of the biological risk factors for violent crime, is it reasonable to assume that the state of anomie that has existed during the emergence of the postindustrial state has led to more biologically based acts of violence? As community control of social norms has been weakened, do the biological risk factors help to explain the sharp increases in the crime statistics?

In large part, it appears that they do not. The biological risk factors that can result in violent behavior and crime—injuries to the cortex and limbic system, depleted levels of serotonin, and some untreatable medical disorders like organic personality syndrome—are few in number, and appear to be generally distributed throughout the population, with small amounts appearing in each generation. For example, serious mental illness usually affects only one percent of any given population of people. While the biological risk factors are important in their own right in individual cases of violence, there is no current evidence that these types of biological factors have substantially increased during the past three decades. It is unlikely that loosened social mores, in and of themselves, would result in increased injuries to the cortex and the like.

Having said this, there may be other ways in which the absence of community may increase certain types of biological risk factors and their interaction with the other types of risk factors. For example, hyperreactivity of the nervous system due to substance abuse by individuals self-medicating the life stress associated with the postindustrial anomie and increased victims of PTSD who subsequently become violent in response to an emphasis on personal entitlement and material gain, are two examples in which biological factors may be exacerbated by the social and cultural dysregulation of our times.

These examples, and there are others, also highlight the importance of the next set of risk factors that we want to examine, the sociological risk factors. The sociological or Nurture risk factors are those factors that are in our environment, and include the physical environment in which we live, the natural resources of the earth, the material resources that we have created through science and technology, and, especially, the presence of others. Humans are social animals who seek to be with others, who cooperate with others for survival, who spend time with others for companionship and the sharing of the journey of life, and we have noted how these caring attachments may become disrupted during periods of great cultural change, such as our own. Of all of the Nurture or environmental resources, other persons appear to have unique importance for human health, human happiness, and the curtailing of violence.

Let us then continue our inquiry into understanding the sociological risk factors for human violence and begin with the factor that medicine and behavioral science tells us is of great importance: other people.

# 3

# NO MAN IS AN ISLAND: SOCIOLOGICAL FACTORS IN VIOLENCE

*The child is father to the man.*
— William Wordsworth

*Humankind . . . cannot endure too much emptiness and desolation.*
— T. S. Eliot

*Dateline: Chicago, Illinois. October 13, 1994.*

*For nearly twenty years lynching crimes . . . have been committed by this Christian nation.*

The two older boys, ages ten and eleven, had much in common. Both had fathers in jail and mothers who could not control them. Both had low intelligence exacerbated by inadequate schooling. Both had seen life's darker side: poverty, guns, drugs, and violence.

*Nowhere in the civilized world save the United States of America do men . . . go out in bands . . . to hunt down, shoot, hang, or burn to death a single individual, unarmed and absolutely powerless.*

Life in the Ida B. Wells housing project on the city's South Side had not been any easier for the two younger brothers, ages five and eight. They and their mother were illegal squatters, three among thousands, in the project's abandoned and boarded up apartments. A waiting list of 30,000 persons offered scant hope of permanent residence. At least, there were heat and hot water, but a squatter's life was makeshift and difficult at best. At times it deadened the soul.

*To our appeals for justice the stereotyped reply has been that the government could not interfere in a state matter . . .*

The five-year-old boy refused to steal candy for the two older boys. Revenge was demanded and the die was cast. The two older boys lured the two younger brothers into one of the abandoned apartments, dangled the five-year-old out the window, and then dropped him to his death fourteen floors below. Five years old. Forty pounds. Sixty miles per hour upon impact. A badly bruised face. Small teeth scattered about. Trails of blood. Massive internal injuries. Dead on arrival.

*We refuse to believe this country, so powerful to defend its citizens abroad, is unable to protect its citizens at home.*

[The italicized quotations in this passage are from the writings of Ida B. Wells, whose name and memory are perpetuated in the housing project where this unspeakable murder took place.]

Violence by children shocks us, but is it new? Writer Patrick Wilson (1975) has compiled a book of over fifty case examples of such murders, primarily in Britain, dating back to 1743. What is new, as noted in chapter 1, is the increasing numbers of violent acts by young people.

Will the sociological risk factors, especially caring attachments to others, help us to understand the increase in youthful crime and similar acts by adults, when there are no apparent, overriding biological causes? Do the sociological risk factors become exacerbated during periods of weakened communities? If they do, how is it that they actually exert their influence on individuals so that they behave aggressively?

Several sociological risk factors were present in the lives of the four youngsters in Chicago: few caring attachments, not enough money, no adult role models, substance abuse, easily available weapons, violence in many forms. While these factors were dramatically evident in the Chicago housing project, they are not limited by social class. These factors with their harmful and aggressive impact are all about us. But why do they result in violence? The disruption of caring attachments may help us understand why this happens.

Medicine and behavioral science have known for some time that disruptions in caring attachments to others can impair physical and mental health, and lead to aggression in certain contexts. The medical evidence documents the negative impact of lack of human companionship and loneliness in cases of bereavement, divorce, sudden loss, death of a parent, a mobile lifestyle, childhood abuse and neglect, and similar disruptions of human bonds. Loneliness does strange things to people. Loneliness can lead to aggression. Loneliness can kill. John Donne was correct: no man is an island. Consider the following example by psychologist James Lynch (1977) of the power of human touch.

A fifty-four-year-old man lay dying in an intensive care unit in a major medical center. For fourteen days, he struggled for his life in battle with severe cardiac disease. Little was known of the patient other than that he had had a problem with alcoholism. There were no known relatives or visitors who made their way to his bedside during these, his final days.

When it became clear that he would die, the nursing staff turned their attention to making him comfortable as he awaited death. Toward the end, the patient was in a coma, and every muscle in his body had been completely paralyzed by a medication known as *d-turbocuraine*. He breathed with a machine for artificial respiration, and telemetry equipment monitored his vital signs.

The man's heart rate changed dramatically on the telemetry units when a nurse held his hand to comfort him during his final hours on earth. Each contact with the nurse resulted in a stabilizing of the heart's rhythms. Even in a coma, fully paralyzed, and attended to by a relative stranger, the patient's heart responded favorably to human contact.

It should not surprise us that human contact and caring attachments are such powerful regulators of human health and happiness. Most of us feel better when we are with friends, receive reassurance and praise, or feel a sense of belonging. Such phrases as "Absence makes the heart grow fonder," "That was a touching tribute," or "She died of a broken heart" reflect this need.

Caring attachments or human bonds are one of our unique attributes as a social species, and, with the exception of freely chosen solitude, most daily activities and major life events actively involve interaction with others. As we shall see, most human problems are best encountered with the support of others.

What is equally important is that the absence or disruptions of these attachments may lead to violent crime. This is a complicated process and is the subject of this chapter. The example of violence in the housing project that we just read may provide us with some initial insights into this process of disruption. What can we say about the caring attachments of the four youngsters at the Ida B. Wells housing project? Were their attachments helpful or harmful? Certainly the older boys had apparently limited contact and support from their parents. While the family of the younger brothers was more intact, for all four youngsters there was a general absence of caring attachments in the form of extended families, teachers, recreational aides, school counselors, and the like. In addition to the absence of attachments, these youngsters were exposed to the sociological risk factors of poverty, guns, drugs, and violence toward others. Violence was the outcome.

Violence occurs when meaningful human contact has failed. This is further exacerbated in the presence of the other sociological risk factors. Since we live in an anomic age when such attachments and contact are often disrupted, we begin our inquiry there. To understand how caring attachments become disrupted, we need to understand clearly how they are formed, and we begin at the beginning with the development of the earliest roots of caring attachments. The process is known as bonding and is present at birth.

## The Nature of Bonding and Caring Attachments

### Caring Attachments

Psychiatrist René Spitz (Lynch, 1977) was one of the first to call to our attention the importance of human contact at birth. His studies were the first to reveal in some detail how infants wasted away if they suddenly lost their mothers. Even with adequate nutrition, these infants would refuse in time to eat and then would eventually die. In one of his studies in 1945–46, he followed ninety-one infants raised in orphanages in the United States. All of the infants were well cared for, but they became anxious and depressed, and did not grow as quickly as they should. Thirty-four of them died, especially during the last trimester of their first year of life.

Unexpected confirmation of these findings came from the studies on primates conducted by psychologist Harry Harlow and his colleagues. His studies began in the mid-1950s and have taught us a good deal about attachments and their disruptions.

In one important study (Harlow and Mears, 1979), Harlow placed two surrogate mothers in a monkey cage. The first surrogate mother was covered with wire-mesh and warmed by radiant heat from a light bulb. The second surrogate mother was a block of wood covered with sponge rubber and terry cloth. It too was warmed by a light bulb behind its head. Both surrogates were constructed so that they could provide milk. Infant monkeys were then placed in the cages. Most chose the surrogate cloth to cling to, even when the wire-mesh surrogate was lactating. When presented with a fear stimulus, most monkeys clung to the cloth mother. When subsequently returned to normal cages with other monkeys, the research animals sometimes displayed autistic behavior and some-times were hyperaggressive. Some later even killed their own off-spring. Harlow understood these findings to suggest the importance of contact and bonding.

In his subsequent research, Harlow studied the effects of mater-nal separation and other social contact in infant monkeys. Infant monkeys were housed in stainless steel chambers without any con-tact with their mother or other animals from birth for periods of three, six, or twelve months. Infant monkeys who spent three months in the chamber were eventually more fearful when released and engaged in less play and exploratory activity, but these effects were reversed fairly soon and normal development continued. Those infants who had been without contact for six months and then were released had infantile responses, no interest in vigorous play, did not know how to protect themselves from aggression by other animals, and were severely socially impaired. Those infants released from iso-lation after one or two years were self-abusive, passive, lackadaisi-cal, and engaged in stereotyped behaviors. Recovery in these last two groups was severely limited, even after several months. Disrupting caring attachments in these primates had serious health and behavioral consequences.

Impressed and understandably concerned with these findings about the importance of early social contact, British psychiatrist John Bowlby (1973) sought to make sense of these research findings and his own observations on humans. He has described what has become known as *Attachment Theory*. Attachment provides the infant with a survival system through its bond with its mother or permanent mother substitute. This link to the caring adult allows the infant protection from predators and permits the infant to learn the activities and skills necessary for survival.

Bowlby also went on to discuss what occurs when the infant/mother bond is disrupted. The break is called *separation anx-iety*. We are all familiar with it as we have all seen infants begin to cry inconsolably when their mothers suddenly leave them to attend to something else. The child cries until the mother returns.

Bowlby noticed that this occurs in a three-stage process: protest, despair, and detachment. The protest phase is marked by anger, thrashing about, and other forms of aggressive and disruptive behav-ior. During this period the infant will cry, look for its mother, refuse to cooperate, will be hostile, and lose sphincter control as the infant is truly in a chaotic frantic state as it searches for its mother. If the mother does not reappear (e.g., as in case of death or prolonged illness), the infant enters into a period of despair that appears analogous to adult grief and mourning. The infant appears sad, withdrawn, and listless, and is uninterested in the world around it. In time, the infant passes into the third phase, detachment, where he or she has minimal interaction with others and with the world. This detachment appears to be a defense against being abandoned a second time.

Repeated findings in research studies (Bowlby, 1973; Lynch, 1977) demonstrate the power of caring attachments in infants to result in health, cooperative behavior, and well-being. Similarly, the research findings document the negative outcome of separation or disruption of these bonds. Health is impaired; aggression may be present; and depression follows, at times culminating in death.

In my own earlier twelve-year study of Stress-Resistant Persons (Flannery 1990, 1994), I found similar evidence for the importance of human contact in adolescents and adults.

When we are in caring relationships with other persons, there are remarkable health benefits for both parties. The presence of caring others may stabilize and strengthen heart rate, and stabilize and lower blood pressure, not inconsiderable benefits in a nation where heart disease is a leading killer. Similarly, the human immune system is strengthened. This is the part of our body that fights some diseases by directly eliminating germs that enter our bodies. A third benefit is that human touch and caring attachments increase the functioning of the body's endogenous opioid system. The opioids are chemicals in the brain called *endorphins* and *encephalins*. The substances circulate in the brain and minimize feelings of pain and depression, as well as make us feel content.

In addition to these important physical health benefits, caring attachments also produce equally important psychological benefits. Our helpful social interactions with others can be grouped into at least four types of beneficial encountering.

(1) First is the provision of emotional support. We have a chance to share our feelings, to minimize our sense of being alone, and to gain courage to go on. (2) Social companionship is a second important benefit in caring attachments. Companionship reduces the loneliness that in extremes can kill, provides meaning for the events of everyday life, and allows us to share the human journey with others and create a common history. (3) Information is the third benefit.

The postindustrial state is highly complex, the range of life choices before us is extensive, and the solutions to life's problems are often complicated. In caring attachments built on trust, we learn from one another. We receive suggestions about possible good courses of action to follow and how to solve particular problems. (4) Finally, caring attachments provide us with instrumental support, tangible offers of help in dealing with life stress. These might include offers of money, material goods, and political favors.

As with the research on infants and children, my research on adolescents and adults suggests that caring attachments improve physical and mental health, and that cooperative behavior with others reduces the stress of life and decreases the risk of violence.

### Disrupted Attachments and Aggression

There is extensive behavioral science literature noting the association between disrupted attachments and aggressive or violent behavior [e.g., see Durkheim (trans. 1951) or Sagan (1987)]. Let me cite a few examples here to show the power of this phenomenon and its presence across the life span.

Canadian psychiatrist Thomas Verny (1981) has written a remarkable book about the events in the mother's life that can affect the development of the fetus. He cites the example of pregnant women who were asked to be still for twenty minutes on an ultrasound table. They were then told that their fetuses were not moving, a normal outcome from the mother's lying still. Most of the women reacted in terror and within seconds the fetuses would be stirring in response to the mothers' fears. Dr. Verny suggests that findings such as these may influence the bonding process in negative ways *in utero* in cases where the pregnancy is unwanted or the mother-to-be has been subject to physical abuse during the pregnancy. Such an intrauterine environment might predispose the child to subsequent lower thresholds for hyperreactivity, including states of aggressive behavior. Verny presents strong suggestive evidence that both helpful and harmful attachments may begin even before birth.

The writings of Spitz (Lynch, 1977) and Bowlby (1973) have provided us with evidence that infants manifest both hostility and aggressive behaviors when their attachments are disrupted, and psychologist Carol Widom (1992) has offered an impressive array of research findings on the impact of violence on young children and their subsequent growth. Her work examines *the intergenerational transfer of violence*, a process by which violent behavior occurs in subsequent generations of the same family.

Parents often have limited coping skills in the face of life stress and conflict. As frustration from the unsolved problems increases, some of these parents use violence against their own children. This violence may take the form of physical or sexual abuse, neglect, or emotional abuse. Widom has been examining what happens when these children become adults, and her results are not encouraging. As these children grow, over one-third of them go on to be abusive themselves in their own families and in their neighborhoods and communities. Violence has led to violence in the next generation. Widom has been studying the possible mechanisms of this generational transfer, and has reached a preliminary conclusion that it is not the violence per se which causes subsequent aggression, but that it is the individual's past history of child abuse along with that person's present life stress and inadequate coping skills that can lead to violence.

As noted in chapter 1, Émile Durkheim has made extensive statistical analysis of suicide and criminal behavior in a variety of countries that were experiencing anomie, or the disruption of the normal social contexts that in turn disrupted caring attachments. Similarly, Lynch (1977) has examined the data specific to the marriage bond as a central human attachment. His review clearly documents that single males have more impaired health and a shorter life span, and that the unmarried have sharp increases in death rates due to motor vehicle accidents and "accidental fires." His studies reveal that white male widowers have a fivefold increase in suicide when compared to married white males as well as a similar dramatic rise in homicides.

Thus, the bulk of the research evidence across the life span offers strong evidence that disrupted caring attachments may result in violence against the self or others.

Although it is true that these findings are sobering, it is also true that there are several studies that suggest these negative consequences of disrupted attachments can be mitigated and in some circumstances reversed.

Over twenty-five years ago, Dr. Bowlby suggested that the negative effects of disrupted attachments could be offset if the infant or child were placed in a familiar environment with familiar persons and possessions and if the mothering care were provided continuously by the same maternal substitute.

Dr. Leonard Sagan (1987) has provided a dramatic example of how powerful this solution to the problem can be. He reports on a study of twenty-six one-year-old institutionalized children whose biological mothers had an average intelligence level of seventy (mild mental retardation) and who had to give their children up for adoption. Half of the children were randomly assigned and placed on a hospital ward for mentally retarded adults. Each of these children was specifically assigned to one retarded adult woman who assumed a motherly role. The remaining half of the children were assigned to routine institutional care.

TABLE 1

**Sociological Risk Factors in Human Violence:**

Poverty

Domestic Violence

Discrimination

Inadequate Schooling

Substance Abuse/ Easily Available Weapons

The Media

Three years later, the latter group had deteriorated in general functioning, and their intelligence level had dropped an average twenty-six points to severe retardation levels. The youngsters who had been assigned specific adult caregivers, however, had significant gains in general functioning and problem solving and their intelligence had increased by twenty-nine points. Thirty years later, those with the caring attachments in youth were more self-supporting and most had completed high school. In contrast, the children without the maternal figures in their lives were primarily still institutionalized as adults, functioning at a third-grade level, and several had died prematurely. Caring attachments by individuals even with limited intellectual skills themselves accounted for these beneficial outcomes.

Noted child psychologist Jerome Kagan (Kagan and Zentner, 1996) recently reviewed all of the studies in which researchers sought to establish predictors for later adult faulty coping and behavior. Like the Sagan example that was just cited, his conclusions are encouraging. Whereas attachments are important, their absence or disruption does not necessarily mean that disrupted functioning, including aggression and violence, must follow. Like Dr. Widom's studies of the intergenerational transfer of violence, the situation is more complex than disrupted attachments in and of themselves. Dr. Kagan found at least three independent factors that must be considered before a particular act of violence might occur. First is the temperament of the child. Children who are relatively calm and develop effective coping styles will usually do well. A second factor is whether the child is in an environment where any psychological vulnerabilities will be exacerbated. The third factor is any consideration that needs to be given to any particular specific life stress situations.

This body of research evidence supports the postulation of Dr. Bowlby that the negative effects of disrupted attachments can be corrected. Creating a familiar environment with the needed resources for growth and basic problem-solving, along with the presence of consistent caring attachments, can be helpful in offsetting these potential negative impacts. While creating this remedial environment is more difficult in an age of great social change and anomie such as the present, the research evidence clearly suggests that it can still be accomplished.

## Sociological Risk Factors in Violence

Having examined in detail the sociological risk factor of disrupted caring attachments and its links to violent behavior, let us consider some of the other sociological risk factors that are commonly associated with violent crime. These include poverty, discrimination, domestic violence, inadequate schooling, substance abuse, and the impact of the media, and all of them may weaken the sense of community. Since these risk factors are reported frequently in the news and are familiar to us, our summary of these factors will be brief, and will focus primarily on how these risk factors compound the problem of disrupted attachments and increase the risk of violence, components in these sociological risk factors that are commonly overlooked.

As we begin, we need to note that each of these topics is a book in its own right. The research findings in each of these areas are complex, often involve the interaction of several factors, may contain subtle nuances, and, at times, are fully conflicting. A discussion of these complexities is beyond the scope of this chapter, but research into these matters is ongoing and the interested reader may want to consider the following books for a deeper consideration of these topics (Biscup and Cozic, 1992; Derber, 1996; Eron, Gentry, and Schlegel, 1994; Flannery, 1992, 1994; Fortune, 1995; Prendergast, 1996).

## Poverty

Our discussion in chapter 1 of the emergence of a permanent underclass without the skills for the postindustrial state reflects an additional face in the continuing problem of poverty. Poverty is here defined as not having adequate income to provide the basics in life such as food, clothing, and shelter. Those with disease, disability, lack of education, or blocked opportunity constitute the poor.

The Roman author Cassiodorus noted long ago that poverty is the mother of crime. This observation has been confirmed repeatedly. It was included in the findings of a presidential commission in the 1960s that was convened to address the causes and prevention of violence. The commission observed that young, poor, undereducated males in oppressive neighborhoods were at high risk to commit crime, especially if they saw others using illegitimate means to acquire material goods. This observation remains true thirty years later for both young men and young women who are poor. Here, we want to examine the concept of the oppressive neighborhood for possible help in understanding how poverty and the presence of disrupted caring attachments interact.

While some poor people, usually sustained by strong religious faith, do succeed without traditional opportunities for education and employment, many do not and find themselves in the oppressive neighborhoods noted by the commission. Here we find the broken homes, disrupted families, and inadequate parenting and schooling that we noted were the common lot of the criminals whom we reviewed in chapter 1. In poor neighborhoods, parents are often absent because of divorce, abandonment, incarceration, addictions, and the like. Of those parents who remain, many are uneducated themselves, and provide inadequate role models for skills learning, verbal conflict resolutions, support, and concern for others. Discipline is often harsh, erratic, or nonexistent so that young people are largely left to fend for themselves.

Working and middle-class families move from such neighborhoods, and local businesses follow suit. The resultant decline in the tax base leads to additional neighborhood problems that include inadequate schools, fragmented health services, and governmental social services that become overwhelmed.

Life in these unpredictable communities leads people to withdraw from others to prevent further disappointments, to replace human contact with material goods, and to emphasize a sense of survivorship that precludes adaptive interaction and reliance on others.

As noted in chapter 1, individuals and families marked with these disrupted family and neighborhood caring attachments are involved in a vast array of the violent crimes that we have studied.

## Domestic Violence

Domestic violence is the commission of violent crimes against one's loved ones. It is found in all age groups, both genders, all races, all ethnic groups, and *all* social classes. By definition, it destroys caring attachments, and frequently results in the aftermath of psychological trauma discussed in chapter 2.

Physical abuse, sexual abuse, nonverbal intimidation, and verbal abuse constitute the main type of traumatic violence that occur in homes. Physical abuse includes the battering of one's spouse, children, step children, parents, siblings, or more distant relatives. Sexual abuse includes rape in marriage, incest by parents and siblings, and occasionally forced prostitution of the children by the parents or stepparents. Nonverbal intimidation covers a variety of noninterpersonal acts and behaviors that are meant to frighten others, such as pounding on the wall in anger. Verbal assaults are verbal threats or statements of intent to harm others. Since these syndromes have been described in detail elsewhere (Flannery, 1992, 1994; Prendergast, 1996), two common examples will be briefly noted here.

Spousal abuse is the battering of one partner by the other. It often includes abuse in the form of derogatory comments and physical assaults. However, it is not limited solely to these methods. Cases have been reported where the instruments of attack have included such things as knives, guns, baseball bats, high-heeled shoes, ashtrays, lit cigarettes, scissors, cords, ropes, doorknobs, acid, bricks, and motor vehicles. Battery in marital rape has included sadomasochistic acts, forced group sex, foreign objects inserted in the vagina, the use of cattle prods, and forced sex with animals.

Domestic physical abuse is cyclical in nature and has three stages that have been identified by psychologist Lenore Walker (Flannery, 1992, 1994). The first stage is known as the tension-building phase and refers to a situation in the home where the batterer is becoming more tense and irritable. The spouse senses this increased vigilance and the inevitable outbreak seems imminent. During the second phase, the violent outburst does, in fact, occur. The victim is threatened, stalked, attacked and mentally tortured in any of the ways noted above in an episode of rage that can last from a few minutes to hours or even weeks. In the third phase, the batterer becomes contrite, begs for forgiveness, and promises that it will never happen again. The terrified, battered spousal victim wants to believe that the nightmare is over, accepts the apology, and the cycle begins again. As the years pass, violence becomes a regular visitor in the home. The frequency of attacks increases and the severity of these episodes escalates. The ugliness in some cases may result in violent death.

Incest is a second unacceptably common type of domestic violence. Human love often attains its most powerful expression of compassionate caring for another in the gift of one's sexuality. Incest is a violation of this boundary, a theft of that special gift, from a child by its parent, stepparent, siblings, or other extended family members. The parental protection and love that should be freely given becomes contingent on sexual favors from the child.

While there appear to be several pathways to family incest, psychologist Denise Gelinas (Flannery, 1992, 1994) has described one of the more common ways in which this may occur.

In some families, the father feels entitled to be waited on. He is frequently the victim of abuse in his childhood and has a basic fear of being abandoned. Commonly, these individuals self-medicate these dysphoric feelings of their childhood with alcohol. In these same families, we find mothers who also were victims of abuse in their childhoods, and who were "parentified" or forced to take up the responsibilities of raising the family because one or both of their own parents refused to do so. These women, too, are fearful of being abandoned and seek some marriage situation where their needs for love and affection will be more adequately addressed.

A man with this background is drawn to a "parentified" woman because she provides for his nurturant needs. The woman for her part is drawn to the man in hopes that her needs for love and loyalty will be met. In fact, such marriages are often reasonably satisfactory during the early years. However, when the first child is born, the "parentified" mother is apt to feel overwhelmed by new caretaking demands. As further children are born, the situation becomes an unendurable burden and the mother often psychologically withdraws from her husband and the children. The husband, fearing rejection, reaches out to one of his daughters for the affection that is no longer being provided by the spouse. In time, it escalates into sexual behavior, which may include intercourse. The overwhelmed mother may or may not know about the abuse, but senses the rejection by her husband. This increases her fears of rejection and abandonment, and she withdraws even further from the family circle.

Does the disruption of caring attachments in domestic violence lead to subsequent crime? The research of Dr. Widom (1992) clearly demonstrates the intergenerational transfer of violence that frequently occurs.

### Discrimination

Discrimination forms the basis for acts of hatred committed against innocent fellow-citizens who are singled out for this violence because of some aspect of their personhood such as race, ethnicity, age, gender, sexual preference, religious beliefs, or medical or psychiatric disabilities.

These citizens find themselves excluded from equal opportunities in employment and housing, from basic freedoms to come and go as the please, and from education and other basic civil rights. The laws and institutions of our neighborhoods and society do not provide equal opportunity, justice, honesty, respect, and tolerance for these victims of discrimination. Moreover, many of these groups are also confronting poverty, inadequate schooling, and underemployment.

These blocked opportunities and the social ills accompanying poverty result in the disruption of caring attachments in family units as well as in the neighborhoods, and are linked to violence in at least two ways.

The first way includes being victims of violent crime at the hands of neighbors. These hate crimes may include verbal harassment and derogatory speech, physical assault, rape, robbery, torture, homicide, and the like.

Often these crimes are committed by persons for whom the American Dream has not materialized, and increasingly this group includes the country's youth. These individuals are personally affected by the changing postindustrial conditions. They are unable to attack the global economy or corporate downsizing so they displace this anger on someone who is different. To inflict pain on one of these innocent victims is to exact economic revenge or to create the illusion of being a powerful person in the face of the assailant's own poor sense of mastery and often the assailant's own feelings of self-hatred. Instead of joining forces in a common cause to act as a counterweight to the prevailing economic order, the perpetrators of hate crimes keep the country divided and distracted from its real problems, and, in doing so, make their own situation worse.

A second way in which victims of discrimination by society at large become victims of violence is at the hands of their own group members. In these cases, fellow victims of discrimination displace their anger at the larger society onto their own group members. Unable to confront the larger social ills, they create the illusion of control and self-direction by committing crimes of assault, rape, and robbery on individuals whom they can confront. These types of crimes are common among some races, some ethnic groups, and those with psychiatric disabilities.

## Inadequate Schooling

Schools provide the opportunity for a community of caring attachments outside the home that continues and reinforces the educational building blocks begun by the parents. In such settings, teachers continue the skills building begun at home, provide extracurricular activities for physical and personal growth, and provide a socialization process that enhances caring attachments by teaching tolerance, discipline, character, and delay of immediate gratification for the pursuit of more helpful long-term goals.

In many parts of our country, however, these basic caring school communities are greatly impaired and the sense of community is weakened. Physical plants are deteriorating, basic supplies and equipment are inadequate or absent, and in some school systems there are not even enough teachers for each classroom.

For their part, teachers themselves must be able to focus on educating students in content areas, but often today's teachers are asked to be police officers, nurses, counselors, and parental surrogates. Teaching is not effective when the students come to class with social problems that the teacher cannot be expected to resolve. These include students with two-career parents, single parents, drug-addicted parents, no parents, different languages and cultures, hunger, illnesses, foster homes, no homes, mental illness, substance abuse, and lethal weapons, either for predatory behavior or self-defense from predatory behavior. [Educator Jonathan Kozol (1991) can provide the interested reader with a detailed discussion of these and other current school system issues.]

Moreover, in many communities the curriculum remains out of date due to an overemphasis on Taylorism. Several decades ago, Frederick Taylor, an automotive industry specialist produced a high school curriculum designed for the industrial state. It provided each graduate with the basic skills for a variety of manufacturing jobs as well as the proper attitudes for good citizenship. Many schools across the country quickly adopted Taylor's approach. The emergence of the postindustrial state has rendered much of this approach impractical, yet many schools retain aspects of Taylorism, and no agreement on a new national curriculum has been adopted.

In addition, there are no national standards, no systems of accountability, no principles of sound fiscal management, and no agreement on lengthening the school year so that needed skills can be learned.

In the absence of coordinated, caring school communities, it should not surprise us that crime is becoming more frequent. Students prey upon students in acts of property theft, rape, and assault. Conflicts between students deficient in verbal conflict resolution skills end in homicides, and assaults and property theft and damage by students on teachers and principals continue unabated.

### Substance Abuse/Easily Available Weapons

Substance abuse, including the abuse of alcohol, is on the rise in our society. Different people use drugs for different reasons. For example, middle-class persons may use drugs to self-medicate the distress associated with the pressures of daily life in an age of anomie. Poor people often use drugs because it is an expected part of daily life, a way to blur the inability to attain the good life, and sometimes because it is also a way to earn a living.

Drugs are being used by parents, teachers, employees, managers, government leaders, ministers, doctors, and others. Since substance abuse can result in brain chemistry changes that lead to violence, as we have seen, it should not surprise us that caring attachments at home, school, work, and the like are being compromised by the presence of these foreign substances in the brain. Alcohol and other drugs are often present in acts of domestic battering, violence in the workplace, community crime, and suicides—events that provide us with painful evidence of how these substances can disrupt caring attachments.

Much of this increased use of drugs and resultant violent crime is related to the emerging drug culture. The risk of violence in the drug culture occurs primarily for three reasons. First is the direct pharmacological effect of many of these agents that result in behavioral toxicity and often accompanying aggression. A second type of violence occurs in the drug industry itself. The distribution of drugs involves turf wars over markets for sales, and violence in the collection of bad debts by drug users. A third source of violence results from the need of the drug user to obtain the money to purchase the drugs. Muggings, convenience store hold-ups, and stealing from one's loved ones are common ways such money is obtained. These three types of interactions result in a system of violence that creates its own arms race where everyone is armed to conduct business or for self-protection. Easily available firearms are employed for material gain, to eliminate witnesses, to frighten others, and to enhance self-esteem. The result is a culture that has more firepower than the police that are assigned to protect the neighborhoods where the drug dealers are, and a culture where arguments instigated over women, material possessions, and even dirty looks are settled by the firing of weapons.

Finally, we should note that the drug lords who run the drug industry capitalize on the disrupted caring attachments found in many of the young in their neighborhoods. These teenagers and younger children are hired to be couriers of the drugs and monies involved in these drug sales. These young people, who do not have the skills needed for traditional employment, can make more money on the street in the drug trade than in some menial entry-level service position. They are seduced by glamor, excitement, and money into a life of crime. Because of the system's violence, most do not expect to live beyond thirty years of age, and many are correct in that assumption.

## The Media

Newspapers, radio, and the early years of television strengthened caring attachments in families and communities by providing large amounts of factually correct information quickly to large numbers of citizens. The result was family and neighborhood discussions of social issues, policies and positions of political leaders, and cultural events that bound people together and strengthened the sense of communal purpose.

In the last thirty years, technology has eclipsed these early beginnings and created a global communications village which includes television, videotapes, AM/FM and shortwave radio, compact discs, cellular telephones, E-mail, and the Internet. This vast expanse of media formats has significantly increased competition for the viewer's attention, and often sexual and aggressive themes are used to draw that attention. This technology also tends to isolate individuals as they frequently engage in these activities by themselves.

These same thirty years have also seen the rise of the working two-parent family and of the single-parent family. The demands of work and everyday life have increased substantially, so that less time is available for childrearing, and some of that time is occupied by television viewing by the children. During these hours, children are exposed to vast amounts of violent episodes of homicides, man-made explosions, car crashes, and the like. With parents absent, no adult is there to monitor the programming itself, or to make sense of why such violence is occurring.

Does violence in the media lead children to behave aggressively?

Of the various media, television violence has been the most studied in detail, and it has been shown in some cases to have a negative impact on children (Wekesser, 1995). In one study in a small town in Western Canada, levels of violence in first- and second-graders were measured after television had been introduced to this isolated community. The study found an increase of 160 percent in the levels of hitting, biting, and shoving by the children within two years of the introduction of television. Other studies report similar types of findings (Wekesser, 1995).

While these findings should alert us to the possible negative impact of violence in the media, the situation is more complicated. Clearly, not all children who watch television become violent, and children in other countries watching the same programming do not necessarily become violent. Children (and adults) have different ways of responding to the violent act. Some may be frightened and not perceive it. Some may turn it into a fictionalized account. Some may become disgusted, and some may imitate the violence. It is this last category, where the child identifies with the aggressor, that needs further study. Television and the other media do appear able to stimulate violence in a child or adult who is predisposed. The predisposing factor(s) elude us at the moment.

As we conclude our review of the sociological risk factors for violent crime, let us ask ourselves the same question that we had of the biological risk factors: Is it reasonable to assume that the anomie associated with the postindustrial state has led to more sociological based acts of violence? As the sense of community has weakened, do the sociological risk factors explain in part the sharp increases in the crime statistics that we studied?

Whereas the biological risk factors did not appear to account for measurable increases in crime, the sociological risk factors do. This is not an unexpected outcome, since the cultural and sociological risk factors overlap to some degree. The values, attributes, and customs of a culture are embedded in that society's social institutions, as we have seen. The strength of that culture and the social cohesiveness of its institutions depends in part on caring attachments. As anomie sets in and the institutional rules change, caring attachments are disrupted and the other sociological factors are also affected. Health, education, income, and other aspects of daily life may all be impaired by anomie and may contribute to increased violent crime. It appears reasonable to assume that increases in the permanent underclass, in more widespread substance abuse, and in declining academic achievement may lead over time to the increased violence associated with these sociological risk factors.

As with the biological risk factors, the sociological risk factors appear to interact with other risk factors. In the previous chapter, we saw how biology and cultural risk factors produced hyperreactivity from substance abuse; similarly sociological risk factors can also interact with these other two sets of risk factors as well as with themselves. Our opening example of the young boys in the Chicago housing project illustrates how poverty, discrimination, substance abuse, and disrupted attachments can all exist simultaneously in one social context with an appreciable increase in the risk for violent crime.

### Nature/Nurture Revisited

Let us close our inquiry of the interactive effects of the Nature/Nurture argument by examining its most dramatic effect: the mystery of psychological consciousness. Psychological consciousness refers to those states of psychological awareness that arise from the interface of the social environment and the biological brain. This interaction includes thinking, remembering, problem-solving, dreaming, and assigning meaning to events.

Psychologists Stanley Schachter and Jerome Singer (1962) devised an important experiment that demonstrates this interactive process clearly. Under the pretext of studying a vitamin supplement to improve vision, the researchers took one group of research subjects, gave them an injection of epinephrine, and told them what correct symptoms to expect. A second group of subjects was given the injection, but not told of the correct symptoms. A third group of subjects was given epinephrine but was told to expect incorrect symptoms. Subjects had to wait twenty minutes between the "vitamin" injection and the subsequent vision test. During this period, subjects in the waiting room were exposed to a researcher confederate who created either a happy, carefree, fun waiting period or an angry, disagreeable wait. Subjects became happy or disagreeable depending on the group that they were in. Schachter and Singer concluded that, in the presence of a state of basic biological arousal, the context or environmental setting also played a role in the observed outcome. They documented the interactive effect of Nature and Nurture that gave rise to the psychological ability to assign meaning to an event.

The ability to assign meaning to events and then to respond to those events accordingly is uniquely human. If John brushes into Henry in the corridor and Henry assumes it was accidental, little in the way of consequences will occur. However, if Henry assumes that John's behavior was intentional and meant to humiliate or injure, then the response to the incident may be sharply more aggressive.

This unique capacity for psychological consciousness and meaning-making, coupled with the person's capacity for exercising mastery in problem-solving, form the final set of risk factors, the psychological risk factors, and we turn our attention to these matters next.

# 4

# IN THE EYE OF
# THE BEHOLDER:
# PSYCHOLOGICAL FACTORS
# IN VIOLENCE

*The heart has reasons that reason knows not of.*
— Blaise Pascal

*If you use the weapon of hate,*
*You get hate for a response.*
— Thomas Dooley, M.D.

*Dateline: New York, New York. November 26, 1995:*

On Wednesday, November 22, the day before Thanksgiving and the twenty-third anniversary of the assassination of President John F. Kennedy, a thriller movie opened across the country and within the city. The film portrayed a group of robber arsonists who stole money from subway booth cashiers in the New York City transit system. Based on real attacks in the 1980s, including the death of a female cashier who was the mother of three young children, the film grossed fifteen million dollars in its first five days.

On Sunday of that same Thanksgiving Day weekend, a fifty-year-old male subway cashier with twenty-two years of experience thought about the upcoming holidays and his son's first year of college tuition and volunteered to work an extra shift beneath the streets of Brooklyn.

At 1:40 A.M., a would-be assailant squirted a combustible liquid into the bullet-proof cashier booth, and then lit a match. The immediate explosion rocked nearby apartment buildings above ground, and demolished the token booth as debris was hurled everywhere and smoke rose to the street-level airshafts above. The cashier, who was now a human torch, pounded himself against the stairwell walls to put out the flames as he raced above ground in sheer terror. Finally, he rolled on the ground in a last attempt to extinguish the flames. Had life imitated art?

His struggle to keep death at bay was constant. Lungs seared from smoke inhalation required oxygen from a respirator. Second- and third-degree burns over eighty percent of his body required strong and continuous pain-relieving sedatives. With his protective skin gone and his immune system suppressed, infection was an hourly bedside visitor. His wife and son, a senior in music at a local high school, kept a silent, lonely vigil—disbelieving and repulsed by man's inhumanity to man.

Within weeks, four young male assailants had been apprehended. Robbery had been the motive and, when the cashier refused to open the booth, they were accused of setting him on fire, even as he pleaded for his life. None had seen the new movie, but life had still imitated art.

On December 10, the honest public servant succumbed to the injuries from the explosion.

In the still and darkness of the night, the wailing lament of a saxophone could be heard as the only son practiced for his father's funeral in the morning.

How could this have happened? As we have noted, we often try to comfort ourselves at moments like these by saying to ourselves that these terrible acts were done on impulse, or by criminals, drug addicts, or other persons who somehow seem abnormal. In so distancing ourselves, we create the illusion that those whom we know would not do such things and therefore we are safe. However, this course of reasoning is just that—an illusion. For in reality, with very rare exceptions, the basic psychological processes of these offenders and of ourselves are essentially similar. Consider the following.

Psychologist Stanley Milgram (1963) was interested in studying obedience, since this is a basic structure of social life. Obedience can be exemplary, as in acts of charity and kindness, but also dehumanizing when individuals are obedient in destructive ways that are contrary to all moral codes.

Dr. Milgram designed a study to assess how obedient average, normal citizens like you and me would be if we were asked to do certain painful acts in the name of obedience to society. In one room, Dr. Milgram designed a board to simulate a shock voltage generator. On the board were markers in ascending levels of voltage from 15 to 450 volts. Markers had designators that ranged from "Slight

Shock" to "Danger: Severe Shock." In a second room, he placed a chair with straps to keep an individual in the chair and with electrodes to hook the individual in the chair to the voltage generator in the first room. In fact, they were not connected and there was no voltage at all.

His study was presented as an experiment in assessing how punishment affects learning and this is how it worked. Naive subjects were recruited through local newspapers and direct mail solicitations. When they came to the research laboratory, they met two confederates. One was a young adult who was defined as the scientist conducting the study. A second confederate came as a subject with the naive subject, but always accepted the role of the learner and was strapped into the chair in the other room to receive shocks, if he gave the wrong answers to the learning tasks. The naive subject was assigned to be the teacher. The scientist read a list of words to be learned. If the learner's answers were incorrect, the teacher was instructed to give increasing levels of shock voltage to the learner. Through levels up to 300 volts, the learner was to provide vocal protest; after 300 volts, the learner was to pound the walls as a response to the pain from the shocks. The true purpose of the experiment was to see how obedient the naive teacher would be when instructed by the scientist to continue to administer shock in the face of the learner's protests and cries of pain.

The naive subjects that Milgram recruited were ordinary persons and included forty males between the ages of twenty and fifty, whose jobs included being teachers, salesmen, engineers, laborers, and so forth.

Milgram's findings give cause for concern. Of the forty subjects only fourteen (thirty-five percent) refused to obey the scientist. Twenty-six (sixty-five percent) followed instructions and were obedient in administering what they thought to be painfully high levels of shock. They did this in the face of their own moral codes and with physical signs of extreme tension that included sweating, trembling, stuttering, biting their lips, laughing nervously, and seizures. Milgram later repeated this sort of experiment with a larger pool of naive subjects and found the same high levels of obedience.

Here we have reasonable evidence that ordinary people of average good moral character can engage in aggressive behavior if the circumstances are right. These findings point to the need for all of us to understand the basic steps in psychological reasoning and the point(s) where negative influences may prove harmful.

There are three basic domains of functioning in humans that ensure good physical and mental health, the relative absence of aggression (except in necessary self-defense), and a sense of well-being. These are reasonable mastery, caring attachments to others, and having a meaningful purpose in life. We examined the importance of caring attachments in the last chapter and will focus on reasonable mastery and meaningful purpose in this one. A brief review of the general process of psychological awareness and problem-solving will be followed by a summary of helpful and harmful strategies for mastery, and an examination of the process of meaning, including the issues of evil and free choice. The chapter will conclude with a brief summary of our interdisciplinary overview of violence to see where our inquiry has led.

In reviewing mastery and meaning, we want to reflect on what went on in the minds of the individuals in San Francisco, Framingham, Chicago, and now New York City. What did these assailants think about as they planned their crimes? How did they perceive the moral imperatives of society when they tortured their fellow citizens?

## Mastery

### *The Process of Awareness and Understanding*

The process of being aware of our environment and of knowing how to respond to it (Scherer, Abeles, and Fischer, 1975) is complex and subject to influence at a number of points that may result in aggressive responses.

The initial step by which we become aware of the environment around us is known as perception. Our sense receptors, such as vision, hearing, and smell, gather information about what is going on around us at any particular time. This information is sent to the brain for evaluation. On its way to the brain, the sense receptor information passes through the nerve fibers and synaptic gaps in the body to the brain. Once in the brain, these receptor nerve impulses pass through the limbic system and then to the cortex where this information is evaluated. Here the brain assesses the information, scans past memory for any other relevant or similar experiences with the event at hand. This step is known as cognition. We do not respond to all information in the environment equally. Our perception and cognition are in many ways organized into categories of importance, and we pay selective attention to those things that are of interest. This process also creates particular ways of responding to recurring situations so that we are apt to respond to a current situation based on our past ways of coping with similar situations.

Each of us learns basic values and attitudes over the years as we interact with the environment. These values and attitudes affect perception and cognition in that we become more sensitive to some sense receptor information than to others. For example, if we were bitten by a dog as a youngster, the presence of dogs in our environment at later times may lead to our paying more attention to every movement of the dog, more so than someone else who has not been bitten. Our past perceptions and cognitive experiences with having been bitten have resulted in an attitude that not all dogs can be trusted to be safe. This attitude then shapes how we respond to the animal's presence.

Attitudes are our learned reactions in evaluating events. They include our beliefs about a particular event, our emotional reactions to that event, and our tendency to respond favorably or unfavorably to the event. They are shaped by our own personal experiences of direct acts, by our witnessing what happens to others, and by what others tell us of similar events from their own lives. Attitudes are also shaped in part by our values, which are principles that are intrinsically valuable or desirable. Often these values are derived from moral, religious, or social codes of acceptable behavior, but not always. Values can also be learned from our parents and extended family members, from our teachers and clergy, from our peers, from our neighborhoods, and from personal life experiences apart from the teaching of others.

When this process of perception, cognition, values, and attitudes leads to productive and socially sanctioned responses or interactions with the daily events that life may bring to any of us, the results are most often adaptive and result in cooperative behavior and health and well-being. However, if the steps in the process are not normative, aggression may be an outcome. For example, injuries to the limbic system and the cortex may result in the entire normal process of perception, cognition, and response being altered. Damage to the cortex's inhibitory centers for aggression may result in violent responses. Similarly, a cortex that is hyperreactive because of substance abuse may have altered states of perception and cognition, and may end with dangerous responses toward the self or others.

Finally, values and attitudes that influence response and that are self-ish rather than cooperative may lead to violent outcomes. Nature and Nurture affect psychological functioning.

The way that we comprehend each event and respond to it depends in large measure on the socialization processes that each of us has with the important other persons in our lives. What they teach us about life events and how to respond to those events determines the shape of our character over time. We explored at length in the last chapter how those caring attachments could, and often were, disrupted. We examined how these disruptions could result in aggressive behavior toward others or against the self. Here the focus is on trying to understand the psychological processes that occur between disruption of the caring attachments and the subsequent violence, and how the process of awareness and understanding becomes so harmfully altered. The answer to this question is more easily understood if we are aware of the normal perceptual process of evaluation, response, values, and attitudes that shape socially adaptive behavior, when attachments are not disrupted.

### Stress-Resistant Persons

Each of us knows some men and women who seem happy and pro-ductive. They face life's adversities as we all must, but they seem able to cope with a minimum of distress, ill-health, or aggression. Their sense of well-being soon returns.

I call these men and women *Stress-Resistant Persons*, (Flannery, 1990, 1994). For twelve years, my colleagues and I examined 1,200 middle-class, working men and women who were attending the College of Advancing Studies at Boston College in the evening. They ranged in age from seventeen to seventy-eight. Within this group, we found those effective problem-solvers who could deal adaptively with life stress so that its potential negative impact was minimized and their productive lives could continue. Our studies suggested that stress-resistant persons have at least six effective skills for coping with life's daily events; these findings are listed in Table 1 on the following page.

*Personal Control.* Stress-resistant men or women take the respon-sibility for their own lives. They clearly identify the problems before them, gather information about possible solutions, develop strategies to solve the problem, and then implement a course of action and evaluate to see whether it has worked. This is perception, cognition, evaluation, and response at their thoughtful best. These individuals also know that there are some problems that are beyond their control and they can do nothing to change the situation. In these cases, they change their attitude toward the problem so that the situation becomes less personally troubling to them.

*Task Involvement.* Task involvement refers to personal goals that motivate us to become involved in the world around us. Personal goals vary widely, but common ones include power, fame, fortune,

TABLE 1

**Stress-Resistant Persons:**

---

1. Take Personal Control

2. Are Task Involved

3. Make Wise Lifestyle Choices

4. Seek Social Support

5. Have a Sense of Humor

6. Espouse Ethical Value of Concern for Others

---

status, career growth, rearing one's children, and community projects. As we shall see later, goals that motivate us for the personal well-being of others may be especially important and helpful. Individuals without personal goals easily become bored, restless, depressed, and sometimes violent.

*Wise Lifestyle Choices.* Stress-resistant persons realize that reducing the physiological arousal associated with life stress may result in improved physical conditioning that is associated with better powers of concentration and problem-solving as well as a greater physical resiliency to cope with life's problems. As opposed to those whose lives are hectic, frenetic, and exhausting, these adaptive problem-solvers employ three helpful strategies to remain calm: reduced dietary stimulants, aerobic exercise, and relaxation exercises. Caffeine and nicotine can turn on the body's emergency mobilization systems for addressing a crisis, even when there is no crisis. Stress-resistant persons avoid unnecessary intake of these stimulants. They also know that regular aerobic exercise keeps the mind and the body fit for dealing with everyday events as well as major life issues. Through regular exercise, they train their bodies to be ready for what life may require of them. Similarly, they know that short periods of relaxation each day also reduce the physiology of life stress and can improve the quality of the reasoning process that we have just outlined above.

*Seeking Social Support.* As we have seen, caring attachments can bring physiological and psychological health benefits, and adaptive problem-solvers understand the importance of these attachments and seek them out. Although they may be contemplative at times, they are not socially isolated men and women, and draw on their network of caring attachments for information and support.

*Sense of Humor.* Humor helps to reduce the physiology of stress and helps us to see the inevitable paradoxes and ironies of life, all of which enable us to keep problems in perspective. Stress-resistant persons are aware of this, and use their sense of humor or associate with those who have one.

*Concern for the Welfare of Others.* Even though we live in the post-industrial state with emphasis on technology, self, and material gain, research findings teach us that those who are primarily concerned with the welfare of others have better health and happiness and significantly fewer moments of aggression. While stress-resistant persons work to attain the material gains of our emerging technologies, they have not lost sight of the importance of concern for others, and their actions are guided by principles of ethical concern for everyone whom they encounter.

Stress-resistant persons utilize these six skills to attain adaptive functioning in the domains of mastery, attachment, and meaning. They utilize personal control, wise lifestyle choices, and a sense of humor to maintain reasonable mastery. They employ task involvement, social support, and concern for others to develop and maintain caring attachments. Similarly, they choose task involvement, social support, and concern for others as their avenue for developing a meaningful purpose in life. Their values and behaviors strengthen the communities in which they work or reside.

## Reasonable Mastery

While stress-resistant persons use all of these skills to enhance mastery, personal control, lifestyle choices, and humor are three factors that bear particular relevance to the basic process of psychological awareness, understanding, and response, with which we began this section.

The lifestyle choices keep the mind and body sound, and improve cognitive capacities to understand and resolve problems. The steps in personal control lead to the gathering of information so that courses of action are thoughtful and deliberate, and therefore, more likely to succeed. Humor helps to keep everything in perspective. Life is a mastered challenge and the need for aggressive behavior, other than in situations of self-defense, is minimal.

What happens when these skills are absent?

## Faulty Mastery

While there has been some research on the psychology of the criminal mind (Gilligan, 1996; Katz, 1988; Toch, 1992), more attention has been paid to the biological and sociological risk factors. Therefore, in this section we explore some of the factors in which there is frequent association between poor mastery skills and violent crime; specifically: weak academic skills, poor interpersonal skills, impulsive behavior, and self-medication to cope with life stress. In this process we are reasoning by inference that these may be psychological causative factors, but the need for long-term prospective studies remains. If it should turn out that these are causative factors, it would help us to understand in part why violent behavior is increasing across all social classes.

1. *Academic Skills.* As we have seen, personal control is our ability to shape the environment to meet our needs. As things become increasingly complex and as the available jobs in our knowledge-based, postindustrial society emerge, it is clear that academic skills are a key component for success. We all know of incidents where students have been unable to answer basic questions in geography and history and have been unable to balance a checkbook or to read the labels in a grocery store. Are these the relatively few failures of the system or are they signs of more deeply entrenched problems?

To assess these matters, the National Institute of Education funded a project known as the National Assessment of Educational Progress (NAEP), (Foster, Siegel, and Landes, 1994). This survey assesses basic competencies among elementary, middle, and high school students. Its most recent survey of 140,000 students in the fourth, eighth, and twelfth grades was conducted in 1992, and its results are not encouraging.

In reading skills, fifty-nine percent of fourth graders, sixty-nine percent of eighth graders, and seventy-five percent of twelfth graders scored at the basic level of competency or beyond, which means they had a partial mastery of the knowledge and skills necessary for reading. While other students were proficient or superior in performance, there are a large number of students at or below the needed reading skills to earn a living and conduct the day-to-day business of life.

In math, thirty-three percent of students in grades four, eight, and twelve were at or below basic levels, again indicating only a partial mastery of the needed knowledge and skills for math. Although most could add and subtract, fewer could do multiplication and division, and even fewer were proficient in fractions, decimals, percents, and general problem-solving ability.

Matters were not much better in writing performance. American students do not write enough and, while they tend to be creative, their essays are often disorganized and without sufficient analytic content.

These findings do not reflect an emerging workforce that is prepared for the jobs that are available. They also allow that, without some remediation, some of these undereducated students may turn to aggressive and criminal behavior in the face of the stress of being unable to obtain adequate and socially acceptable methods of earning a living.

2. *Interpersonal Skills.* While disruptions in caring attachments can leave us without companionship and with feelings of loneliness and social isolation, disrupted attachments also leave us without role models from which to learn the interpersonal skills not formally taught in school. Broken homes and dysfunctional families are not helpful for learning about how to trust others. The simple principles of predictable behavior and similar values (Flannery, 1990, 1994) are not understood and the foundation for trust is not established. Indeed, erratic behavior on the part of

parents in the areas of sharing, discipline, and emotional support may result in deceitfulness.

These children also fail to learn important lessons in cooperative behavior. Parents, extended families, and community caretakers are needed to teach youngsters to share, to support others, and to resolve life's inevitable disagreements with verbal conflict-resolution skills rather than with violent behavior.

Related to this is the absence of empathy in youngsters who are not taught how to cooperate. Cooperation is necessary for survival and a key component in cooperative behaviors is empathy or the ability to understand how another person feels because of our behavior or some other painful life event. Parents need to teach children how others feel when loved ones die or are sick, when plans fall apart, or when the child's rude, angry, or selfish behavior negatively affect others. When empathic skills are not taught, we end up with adolescents and young adults who victimize others and have no sense of remorse (Gilligan, 1996).

The absence of trust, cooperative behavior, and empathy are often seen in personal entitlement and in patterns of material acquisition where self-gain is promoted first at any cost.

3. *Impulsive Behavior.* When individuals grow up in environments of continuous change due to broken homes, dysfunctional families, inadequate parenting and/or widespread poverty, the events of daily life frequently do not follow predictable patterns. The rules of family behavior may vary from one day to the next. If the rules remain stable, the penalties may vary greatly. Expectations are unclear, and acceptable behavior is hard to fathom.

In this type of environment, children and young adults learn that nothing is truly stable, and that one must cope as best one can on an ad hoc basis. One psychological result of all of this is impulsive behavior, which forms the basis of much criminal behavior. People rob, assault, and even commit homicide because they have neither the skills, the time, nor the social resources to find more acceptable solutions for their needs.

4. *Substance Abuse.* As individuals have fewer skills to cope with the complexity of today's societal demands, the levels of stress, frustration, and poor self-esteem increase. In such circumstances, individuals increasingly are turning to alcohol and drugs to self-medicate the negative effects of feeling overwhelmed, hypervigilant, anxious, and angry. Inadequate sleep further compounds

these problems, and many seek drugs as a method of inducing a state of calm and relaxation.

This self-medication can have at least two unwanted results related to aggression. First, as noted earlier, the entire cognitive process for the psychological processing of information, evaluation, and response is markedly impaired by the presence of these chemical agents. In addition, the person is at high risk to develop hyperreactivity, cortical dyscontrol, and violent responses.

In summary, the lack of adequate academic and interpersonal skills, and the presence of impulsive behavior and self-medication of unpleasant feeling states is far removed from the adaptive mastery skills of stress-resistant persons and places the individuals in situations associated with high risk for violence and crime.

## *Meaningful Purpose*

All of us need a reason to guide our lives, to provide direction in day-to-day tasks, and to fortify our strength in life's darker moments. A meaningful purpose in our lives provides such a compass throughout life. These purposive goals, when they are based on concern for others, often result in better health, increased cooperative behavior, and a sense of contentment, even in the face of adversity.

Such a meaningful purpose emerges from a sense of coherence about life. Sociologist Aaron Antonovsky (1979) has written at length about the sense of coherence. It includes three components that provide us with a world view and with a perspective on human events. The first component is manageability and is rooted in the belief that we can have some reasonable control over our environment and shape it to some degree, so that we can attain some of our goals and needs. The second component is comprehensibility, or the fact that the world has some order and predictability that can be understood with a degree of accuracy and consistency. The third component is the sense of purposeful meaning, a belief that the world is worthy of our investment of energy in it.

A second sociologist, the late Ernest Becker (1973), has presented equally important considerations in developing a meaningful purpose. He has noted that we humans are half spiritual in the sense of psychological consciousness and half animal in the sense that we are biological organisms. Our conscious self understands that our biological self will die, and the conscious self seeks some transcendent meaning of life so that it may be assured that its memory will live on after its physical death. When Becker surveyed the goals that society provides to motivate us, he discounted the overarching importance of power, fame, recognition, material gain, and the like, because each of these is finite and ends with the death of the person who has acquired them. They are not strong transcendent foundations for living on in the memories of others.

Better are those goals that link us to others in acts of concern for them—living for others, giving to others, protecting and caring for others, brightening the lives of others. There are many ways to do this, and some of the more common include creating a caring marriage, rearing one's children, joining a helping profession, performing acts of personal charity, or making artistic or creative contributions to community needs. These goals are transcendent in that in life they provide meaning, even in the face of suffering, disability, difficult loss, evil acts by others, and similar forms of tragedy. They are also transcendent in death and act as markers in the memories of others of our own short appearance in the history of the human family.

## Reasonable Meaning

When we were conducting our research studies on stress-resistant persons, we noted their preference for being concerned with the welfare of others. Even though these men and women sought to attain a reasonable share of the world's material goods, power, and recognition, they were primarily guided by an internal compass that sought transcendent meaning. Their transcendent choices primarily focused on task involvement for others, seeking out the social support of others, and being guided by a concern for the welfare of others. This primary concern for others is usually found within the context of the traditional values of hard work, honesty, and self-denial. This primary concern for the welfare of others mitigates against the use of aggression in resolving conflict.

## Faulty Meaning

If individuals do not attain meaningful direction in their lives from helping others or from other socially accepted methods such as fame, influence, and the like, what other choices for meaning might they consider? The more common values and attitudes that people may then choose are listed in Table 2. They are not arranged in any order of importance, but these choices are frequently associated with crime and violence.

Catharsis, or the need to express overwhelming feelings of anger, frustration, sadness, and sometimes depression, may result in aggressive behavior. These violent acts are usually impulsive and are not directed at particular specific individuals. Usually, the victims are the wrong persons in the wrong place at the wrong time.

TABLE 2

**Common Psychological Values and Attitudes in Violence:**

---

Catharsis
Excitement
Enforcement of Norms
Escape
Justice
Religious/Political Belief
Selfishness
Self-Esteem
Self-Expression
Self-Indulgence
Shame
Social Acceptance

---

Generating excitement is another common factor, particularly in robberies. Planning, implementing, and getting safely away from the confrontation is a thrilling experience for some aggressive people. Certain studies suggest that some criminals have low physiological arousal levels, and creating exciting situations may be one way that these individuals attempt to feel more alert.

The enforcement of norms often plays a role in aggression. For example, youth groups often have rules of discipline that require members to commit property crimes or to harm others to gain and then maintain group acceptance. Escape from pressure is another common theme. When some individuals are cornered by life circumstances or by the police, they may become violent in an attempt to flee the immediate stressful situation.

Seeking justice is also a recurring finding in many of these cases. The individual is seeking justice, seeking retribution for perceived undue injustice, or seeking to prevent injustices. In such cases, the individual has taken matters into his or her own hands, and has assumed judicial powers that society collectively entrusts to other societal institutions.

Religious and political beliefs motivate some, and this can be seen fairly clearly in acts of terrorism. The adherents to these various tenets believe in the full truth and justice of their causes and believe that violence as a means to attaining the end of spreading the message is acceptable.

Not surprisingly, selfishness is found in many acts of aggression in our society. The emphasis on personal entitlement, material gain, and a disregard for the welfare of others sets the scene for many acts of interpersonal violence. In this view, others serve as tools for one's personal needs.

Related to selfishness are issues of self-esteem, self-expression, and self-indulgence. In matters of self-esteem, aggression may erupt in the face of threats of inferiority, blame, humiliation, and dependence on others. Aggression by these individuals transforms their sense of insignificance into that of noteworthy power.

Violence related to self-expression may erupt in the face of anger or disappointment at not receiving the expected outcome. It may also be an act of hatred and protest directed at the person perceived to be responsible for the withholding. Sometimes, self-expressed violence is unrelated to loss, but serves as a means of communicating the personhood of the individual who feels the need to reaffirm his or her importance.

Self-indulgence is another form of violence toward others that is perpetrated because some individuals believe that others exist primarily to cater to the assailants' needs. Self-indulgent violence is often present in domestic spousal abuse and in the battering of children by either parent.

Shame and social acceptance are the final categories in Table 2. Many of our hardened career criminals have long histories of severe physical abuse as children. These acts have included events such as being tied up for long periods of time, being locked in closets, not being fed, having no access to toileting, being punished for minor rule infractions by having their wrists cut with a knife, or having their wrists or ankles shot at. Such behavior by parents induces anger in the youngsters, but also profound shame. They come to perceive themselves as inherently damaged goods and a disgrace to the human family. In some of these cases, the violent behavior is a method of being caught and punished not only for the specific crime at hand, but as a deserved outcome for being such disgraces.

Social acceptance is the obverse of enforcing the norms. In the first case, the leaders enforce certain codes of antisocial behavior to maintain leadership and to promote group cohesiveness. In the cases of violence that occur within the context of social acceptance, individuals are engaging in aggression and deviance to be accepted by the deviant group.

The list in Table 2 should not be considered exhaustive of all the possible motives for aggressive behavior, but it does present us with a wide array of possible meaningful purposes that are at variance with society's needs. All of these motives are greatly removed from concern for the welfare of others, and therein lies their common flaw.

The adoption of these various antisocial values and attitudes usually arise when the individual has poor mastery skills and is ignorant of other more socially acceptable solutions to problems. The introduction of these negative values and attitudes creates a psychological process of awareness, understanding, and response that is counterproductive to societal needs and demands, and that inhibits the development of caring attachments. It results in the person being isolated from the more normal set of social expectations and rewards, and frequently concludes with the individual being arrested or incarcerated. The offender, the victims, and society as a whole pay an unacceptably high cost for these types of outcomes.

These values and attitudes differ significantly from the traditional values of cooperative behavior, but are the values increasingly employed by many in this age of anomie.

### Psychological Theories of Aggression

From time to time, certain theorists have tried to build models to explain aggressive behavior. In general, these theories are in need of more empirical testing before they can be accepted completely, but let us review the five that have garnered the most attention.

The first theory of aggression is known as the classical theory and was first formulated by Jeremy Bentham in 1789. Bentham believed that people were motivated to seek pleasure and avoid pain, and that criminal behavior was not different in this respect. Whereas the pursuit of pleasure explained some criminal behavior, the fact that criminal behavior and other forms of violence continued in the face of punishment weakened the theory and led others to seek better explanations for these matters.

The next major theory was Sigmund Freud's instinct theory (Hall and Lindzey, 1957). Freud postulated that each person was born with both life and death instincts. The death instinct was thought to be the goal of all life in that all living things had a tendency to return to the stability of the inorganic world. The aggressive drive was considered self-destructive behavior turned outward against substitute objects. Over time, the death instinct prevailed. As we have already seen, there is little research data to support instinctual theories of aggression.

The third major theory of aggression to emerge was the frustration-aggression hypothesis put forth by psychologist John Dollard and his colleagues (Huesman, 1994). It was Dollard's premise that, when people are thwarted in their attempts to meet their needs and other goals, aggression will follow. Dollard did not believe that aggression was innate in people, but he did assume that environmental stress would lead to violence. Although it is true that some frustrated persons in some situations do strike out, not everyone does. Research on the frustration-aggression hypothesis demonstrated that this relationship was very complex and involved several possible mediating variables as well as outcomes other than aggression.

Psychologist Albert Bandura (Huesman, 1994) took up the challenge of this complexity in his social learning theory of aggression. In his model, violence is considered to be a function of learning experiences from interactions with the environment. This learning can take place by means of direct personal experience or by observing others. Whether one learns to be aggressive depends on whether the aggressive behavior is rewarded or punished. For example, if children observe other children being harmed by a third child, and that third child is never punished for those violent acts, then the children who observed this will tend to have higher probability for behaving aggressively themselves later on. Dr. Bandura singled out the importance of the parents as role models both for teaching socially acceptable behavior and for punishing antisocial acts. As with the frustration-aggression hypotheses, the social learning model could explain some violent acts but not all of them.

Psychologists Leonard Eron and Rowell Huesman (Huesman, 1994), among others, noted that what the individual was specifically thinking when the aggression occurred was a key variable or factor in understanding whether the individual would behave violently. They have developed the most recent theory of aggression, the social-cognitive theory.

Huesman believed that social behavior is controlled in large measure by the individual's past learning experiences. Programs for behavior or ways of coping with life stress, which are called cognitive scripts in this model, are learned and then stored in memory. When a similar situation occurs later in life, the individual recalls the cognitive script and evaluates its suitability for the present situation. Crucial to this process are the values and standards that the individual has learned, which guide that person's actions. A child that does not learn nonaggressive values and attitudes is more likely to select and implement cognitive scripts that result in violence.

As with the previous two theories of aggression, the social-cognitive model allows us to understand why some people behave violently. However, aggression does not routinely occur in the lives of most individuals, so we are in need of a more sophisticated model before we will be able to predict with accuracy who is likely to become violent.

### Evil and Choice

Just as the Nature/Nurture argument has a long history of thoughtful deliberation, there has been a similarly lengthy debate over whether every act that a human performs is a determined function of the laws of Nature (as understood by science) or whether humans have free choice to behave as they wish in their day-to-day lives.

This debate takes on particular importance in our understanding of the accountability for violent acts against others. If we believe that all human behavior is determined by the laws of Nature, then the individual is not personally responsible for the behavior since it is a function of biology, physics, and so forth. If we believe that humans have free choice in how they will behave, then humans are held accountable for their acts. The determinant position is to be found in science, and the free-choice position is embedded in our legal system. Our understanding of these matters is important when we consider the problem of evil.

Evil refers to the morally reprehensible, seemingly senseless acts of destruction that occur at the hands of nature or in the hands of others. Evil is the destruction of the goodness of things, the destruction of the integral properties of inorganic matter, living plants and animals, and humans. This destruction may impair physical integrity, functional abilities, and the basic beauty of the object.

Some evil occurs in natural disasters like volcanoes, floods, and earthquakes. These events are a part of the nature of things as found in the principles of physics and energy in the created universe. Again, victims of these acts are the wrong persons in the wrong place at the wrong time. With the passage of time, victims come to understand the power of nature and move on in life.

Harder to overcome are evil acts perpetrated by human maliciousness. The various acts of violence that we have seen in these pages that have resulted in cruelty cannot be as easily explained away. Murder, rape, robbery, and assault do not seem similar in nature to the randomness of natural catastrophes. In the face of such malice and perversion, finding meaning becomes more difficult in those acts that are not directly attributable to brain injury or undiagnosed medical illness.

In understanding human acts of evil, some find it helpful to believe in fate, and to accept that good and evil are principles in the world that we must accept. Others believe in basic rights for each person or basic ethical principles that require us to treat each other with justice and respect. Still others believe in a loving God who has given humans freedom of choice, a freedom that can be abused if individuals act in ways that are destructive to themselves or others. Each of these views can help us understand the meaning of the horrifying experiences of malice that occur daily in our country, and, to date, the medical and behavioral science literature has provided no consistent evidence that human behavior and choice is fully determined by scientific principles, except in those few cases of brain injury or medical illnesses where the person's process of awareness, understanding, and response has been clearly damaged beyond the person's control.

In closing this review of the psychological risk factors, let us pose the same question that we had of the biological and sociological risk factors. Does anomie and the weakening of community in the postindustrial period exacerbate the psychological risk factors?

The answer is similar to that for the sociological factors in that anomic conditions and the decline of community do provide more opportunity both for the assigning of self-centered, harsh, and harmful meaning to various events and for the choosing of various socially maladaptive responses to these events. Increases in robbery, rape, and hate-based crimes may reflect this association.

The psychological risk factors also can interact with the other risk factors, and with themselves, just as the biological and sociological risk factors may do. For example, substance abuse (sociological) may cause neurological hyperreactivity (biological) which may lead to harsh motives (psychological) toward others. Similarly, poverty (sociological) may lead some to conclude that theft from others is justice attained (psychological).

This interaction effect provides a further array of diversity to the several sets of primary risk factors themselves.

## Violence in America: An Overview

This interdisciplinary review of the biological, sociological, and psychological risk factors that may result in violence in our country is summarized in Table 3 on the following page. It reflects the greater significance of the sociological and psychological risk factors as we have seen.

In order that we will better understand the principles for containment and prevention in part 2, let us review the main points that have emerged thus far.

1. First, violence in America is a major public health problem. It is an epidemic that has spiraled out of control during the past thirty-five years, especially among our country's youth. This violence is as virulent as any virus in destroying the social fabric, and it is at our own peril that we ignore this problem or imagine that it will go away.

2. During this same thirty-five year period, the country has experienced the impact of a major social transformation as we have moved from the industrial to the postindustrial state. This transformation has resulted in cultural anomie and has uprooted our traditional ways of interacting with each other as our basic

## TABLE 3

Possible Risk Factors in Violence:

| Biological | Risk | Sociological | Risk | Psychological | Risk |
|---|---|---|---|---|---|
| Cortex | Yes | *Inadequate Attachments* | | *Inadequate Mastery* | |
| *Limbic System* | Yes | Children | Yes | Academic | Yes |
| | | Adults | Yes | Interpersonal | Yes |
| *Hyperreactivity* | | | | Impulsive | Yes |
| | | *Social Factors* | | Substance Abuse | Yes |
| Bodily States | Yes | | | | |
| Norepinephrine | No | Poverty | Yes | *Meaning* | |
| Serotonin | Yes | Domestic Abuse | Yes | | |
| Testosterone | No | Discrimination | Yes | Values/Motives | Yes |
| | | Schooling | Yes | Evil Behaviors | Yes |
| *Instinct* | No | Substance Abuse | Yes | | |
| | | The Media | Yes | | |
| *Genetics* | | | | | |
| General Personality | No | | | | |
| Traits | No | | | | |
| *Medical Disorders* | | | | | |
| General Conditions | No | | | | |
| Personality Disorders | No | | | | |

social institutions of business, government, the family, schools, and religion are themselves undergoing a period of rapid change. The sense of community has been uprooted, caring attachments to others have been disrupted, and values of hard work, honesty, and self-denial have been replaced by personal entitlement, material gain, and instant gratification.

3. Violence occurs when meaningful human communication fails, and we have examined how the biological, sociological, and psychological risk factors, individually and in interaction with each other, create situations that distance us from one another and further weaken our sense of community.

4. Although there are many determinants that result in violence, most acts of violent crime remain freely chosen. There are only a few medical conditions that precipitate violence and that are beyond the individual's control.

There are several implications of these main points as we approach strategies for intervention and prevention in part 2.

As a nation we need to address the issue of creating and strengthening the sense of community—in families and neighborhoods, in schools, in religion, in government, and in business. Although we cannot preclude the postindustrial transformation, we can be alert to its potential negative effect on the sense of community and the social mores that govern how we interact with one another. Creating and sustaining community is a primary focus in addressing our current levels of violence, just as it was during the period of the 1880s to the 1890s.

Since violence has many potential risk factors, the main points also suggest that we will need a variety of solutions to contain these risk factors. There will be no one answer. Rather, it will depend upon the interests and strengths of all of us in creating a mosaic where the sum of the parts will result in decreased levels of violent crime. Each of our solutions should focus on building bridges and attachments between our fellow citizens, and the element of free choice indicates the potential for individuals to choose more socially acceptable solutions over violence.

One of our strengths as a people has been the ability to find creative solutions in the face of adversity. From the Revolutionary War to our own day, there has been no problem that has completely overwhelmed and incapacitated our countrymen. True, there have been serious setbacks but, over time, the nation has rallied to solve its problems and to move on and prosper. So it can be with the current levels of escalating violence. The collective efforts of each of us to strengthen the sense of community can eradicate the multiple determinants of this present social ill, and reduce our levels of fear and life stress.

Let us close part 1 by examining a fairly recent case that drew national attention because of the horror of the act of violence. Let us consider how our interdisciplinary survey of the risk factors for violence can help us to understand the behavior of a young mother who strapped her two young children into the car seats, drove them to a loading ramp at a lake, and then released the car and the children to roll into the lake and certain death.

### *Dateline: Union, South Carolina. October 25, 1994.*

> In the coolness of an autumn evening, the young mother, twenty-three years of age, strapped her three-year-old and fourteen-month-old sons into the family car. She drove the backroads of Union for three hours before reaching John P. Long Lake, and letting the car, with the two children inside, slide to the bottom of the murky water.
>
> She ran to a nearby stranger's home and reported that she had been the victim of a carjacking by a person of color. For nine days she won national sympathy on television with tearful pleas for the safe return of the boys until she herself confessed that she had arranged the drownings in order to save a romantic relationship with the son of an affluent businessman. The son did not want her as a partner as long as she had children.
>
> The national sympathy turned to horror and outrage as the country learned the truth. It softened somewhat as other facts about the mother became available during the legal proceedings.
>
> She had periods of depression, had apparently tried to commit suicide on two occasions, had a biological father who had committed suicide when she was six and a stepfather who sexually abused her, and found herself in a loveless marriage to the assistant manager of a grocery store.
>
> The jury, the residents of Union, and the citizens of the country pondered whether she was guilty and personally accountable. Did she have the "capacity to conform her conduct to the law"?

From the evidence and statements made public in the various legal proceedings in this case, we learn about the possible roots of her violent actions. Since violence frequently is multiply determined, there may be more than one risk factor to be considered in this case.

From the cultural point of view, we note that the assailant was a young female between the ages of fifteen and twenty-four so that she is considered in the group of citizens increasingly at high risk for committing violent acts. Although she was apparently romantically drawn to the son of a wealthy businessman, she and her husband had good jobs and were not members of the permanent underclass. This suggests that the community schools were adequate in preparing the town's citizens for current gainful employment. Her family life, however, does not appear to have been fully adequate. The family structure was broken by her father's successful suicide when she was six. Home life and parenting were inadequate as evidenced by the sexually abusive behavior of her stepfather. Not enough is known from the public record to gauge the impact of church and government in her life.

Her personal health history may have raised questions for the jury. She was reportedly depressed at times in her life and had made two apparent suicide gestures. Was she psychologically depressed and suicidal that night at the lake? Although it is possible, her calculating lying behavior for the next several days would raise questions about the absence of power to reason. It is unknown from the proceedings whether she suffered from untreated PTSD with kindling.

It is clear that her network of caring attachments was disrupted at least with the males in her life. Her father's suicide, the stepfather's abusive behavior, and the lack of perceived support from her husband that resulted in filing for divorce suggest the loss of important attachments, even as she was able to sustain others. With regard to the major sociological risk factors associated with crime, domestic violence was present, but absent were poverty, discrimination, inadequate schooling, and substance abuse. Any impact of the media on her development is unknown.

In terms of psychological risk factors for these two homicides, she apparently put her needs before those of the children in a self-centered attempt to retain her romantic liaison, but there is no evidence of extensive antisocial behavior and, indeed, there is much data to suggest that she really cared for the children. While her parenting skills were apparently good, her interpersonal skills with males were less than adequate and apparently caused her much unhappiness.

Was she responsible for her behavior and actions at the lake or not? A jury of her peers found her guilty and accountable for her acts. Her personal suffering was a mitigating factor in her sentence of life imprisonment versus death, but she was held responsible for her violent actions.

A violent event with tragic consequences for a small Southern town and for the country at large.

# PART TWO

# VIOLENCE IN AMERICA: SOLUTIONS

# 5

⬦

# RESTORING COMMUNITY: BUSINESS AND GOVERNMENT

*It is the manners and spirit of a people*
*which preserve a republic in vigor.*
— Thomas Jefferson

*Determine that the things can and shall be done*
*and then we shall find a way.*
— Abraham Lincoln

### Dateline: Fort Lauderdale, Florida. February 9, 1996.

The early morning sky was still and full of stars. A southeast breeze gently pushed the ocean to the water's edge. The air temperature was in the mid-sixties and the water temperature was seventy-one degrees. Shortly, the first deep purple bands of sunrise would puncture the darkness of the night. It was a special moment to be alive.

In a nearby temporary trailer, the city's beach cleaning crew was gathering. Known as the Hurricane Crew because of their ability to clear the city's beaches quickly after natural disasters, the several men and one woman, a transfer from the cemetery caretaking division, talked casually as good friends do as they waited for their next assignment. What they did not know was that this would be their last assignment. For most, today would be the day of their death.

"Love to All" reflected the greeting in the window, but inside anger was the coin of the realm for the homeowner and father of three who was an ex-Marine and decorated rifle expert. For eighteen years he had been a member of the Hurricane Crew, but fourteen months ago, he was fired for drug use and for harassing tourists on the beach.

Things had gone downhill from there. New work had been hard to come by. His wife needed surgery and she became unable to work. When his home hot water failed, he had to send his family away temporarily. He was fired from his security guard position last week, and yesterday he had been rebuffed in his efforts to regain his city position at the beach. Home alone, he seethed in anger.

Fourteen months to the day he lost his city post and less then twenty-four hours after he was rebuffed by the city a second time, the ex-Marine decided to return to work one last time. On this still Friday morning at about five o'clock, he stormed the city's beachside trailer. Armed with two handguns and trained thoroughly by the United States Marines, he methodically murdered five of his former colleagues as they frantically sought to escape. Then, he turned the gun on himself.

The City of Fort Lauderdale awoke. Six of its residents were now widows, and several of its children now had only one parent.

Unemployment. Drugs. Rage. Guns. Death. Another American Dream had ended in pools of blood.

The sunrise came in darkness.

Here is a painful example of violence in the workplace. Homicide is the leading cause of death for women at work and the third leading cause of death for men at work (Flannery, 1995). If we were to ask for suggestions about how to effectively address these homicides at work and the other types of violent crime that we have studied, many of us would suggest more police officers, longer prison terms, the interdiction of illegal drugs, and the like. Intuitively we would mention effective ways to address the biological, sociological, and psychological risk factors. While these suggestions would be correct and helpful in part, in the longer term these approaches would not prove to be fully adequate.

If these three sets of risk factors are exacerbated by cultural anomie, then we need to address that matter as well. If periods of great social change alter the rules for how we are to behave and result in the weakening of community and caring attachments such that violence may result, then our approaches for reducing and containing violent crime will need to include programs that both strengthen community in general as well as addressing specific risk factors in particular. Initiatives that emphasize shared social values, active exchange of ideas, and the search for solutions draw citizens together, foster caring attachments, and strengthen community. Such solutions mitigate the sense of isolation, minimize the negative effects of anomie, and reduce crime and violence. We have already seen evidence of the ability to restore attachments and community in the examples noted by Bowlby and Sagan in chapter 3.

In the remaining chapters, we will examine approaches to contain and reduce violence in each of our basic societal institutions.

We want to examine the many ways in which we can empower ourselves as individuals and as communities to cope with the violent crime around us. Some programs will be familiar and will serve to remind us of the basics that create caring attachments and lessen the probability of violence. Others will be new and will demonstrate the power of human ingenuity in finding solutions to a continuing problem.

In selecting these examples, we will focus on the sociological risk factors. The biological risk factors are reasonably constant as we have seen and many can be successfully treated by medicines. The psychological risk factors for revenge and the like often follow from the perception of sociological injustices, so our attention will be directed primarily toward the sociological factors.

In reviewing what thoughtful citizens have been able to accomplish, we depart from the more formal scientific findings. The solutions that are presented here are best thought of as pilot studies to be further tested by other citizens in other parts of the country, so that we can replicate and learn what strategies are the most effective. Thoughtful solutions will emerge through trial and error.

This overview of effective approaches can also serve as a stimulus to our own sense of creativity. What are our personal strengths? What are our areas of community interest? Where can our efforts make a difference in strengthening the sense of community? Perhaps in individual cases, some will emphasize better parenting, more active school involvement, or a particular neighborhood project. Our solutions will need to be effective and consistent with what we can afford, but our creativity in this search should remain unfettered.

The guidelines and examples presented in these next two chapters are by no means exhaustive. Additional resources and help may be found in Appendix B, the select list by topics of national associations involved in reducing violence. These selected societies cover many issues and are valuable resources for reading materials, for information on proven strategies, and as important networks for linking individuals drawn to common problems. Those individuals interested in starting community initiatives will want to learn what legal or liability issues may be involved. Consulting with the appropriate national associations, as well as with federal, state, or local government agencies, may prove helpful in this regard.

In this chapter, we focus on helpful initiatives in business and in government.

## Business

Business can make important contributions toward coping with violence in at least three important ways. The first is to be a well-run, growing, profitable company. Profitability immediately strengthens individuals, families, and communities through payroll expenditures and taxes, and profitability in the longer term permits companies to be socially responsive to basic community needs. Secondly, business can also be of assistance in developing company policies and programs that are family-friendly for their employees and that assist employees in finding needed balance in today's age between work and family. Finally, some companies become involved in supporting specific programs that address specific risk factors associated with violence. Each of these three approaches fosters caring attachments, strengthens community, and lessens anomie.

In considering these business approaches, it may be helpful to consider how we might become active in these types of interventions as chief executive officers (CEOs), as managers, as employees, as customers who support helpful companies, and as neighbors who may want to request financial support for a charitable project.

### Strengthening Community: Basic Approaches

*The Role of Profitability.* A profitable business is an asset that strengthens the community where it is located. By employing local residents, purchasing supplies from local merchants, and supporting city services through tax levies, business strengthens the attachments in neighborhoods and communities. Such approaches not only maintain an adequate quality of life, but also contain violence by precluding possible increases in membership in the permanent underclass, at least with respect to its own employees.

This mainstay of the community continues to function quietly each day. Its important role in containing violence is rarely thought of until the business falls upon hard times or closes. All of us know of cities and towns across the country that have been devastated when local businesses have closed or moved away. More often than not, these abandoned communities then face economic downturns, increases in social welfare costs, and, in some cases, increases in violent crime.

Occasionally, this quiet, daily process of community support is highlighted by some major tragedy that demonstrates its importance. Consider the following.

### Dateline: Lowell, Massachusetts. December 11, 1995.

They gathered in a Boston restaurant to honor a decent and God-fearing man on his seventieth birthday. It was a fitting tribute to the compassion and goodness of the chief executive officer of a fabric company.

His company produced eighty percent of the fleece fabric for outdoor clothing, a fabric manufactured from recycled materials, and the business was highly profitable. Thus, it seemed fitting to honor the owner in the twilight of a long and distinguished career.

The call came at midnight. There had been a terrible fire. Over thirty employees had been injured. Some seriously. For sixteen hours in forty-five-mile-per-hour winds in the dead of winter, the fire storm raged. It was feared that all was lost.

Arriving at his factory, the owner steeled himself. No tears would be permitted.

He drew strength from his Jewish faith, particularly from Micah 6:8: "He has told you, O Man, what is good and what God really wants from you: Only that you act justly, with loving kindness, and walk humbly with thy God."

But where to begin?

Gathering his several thousand employees, he announced that all of them would be salaried for the next thirty days and have health benefits for the next ninety days. His customers agreed to wait until the plant was up and running again. Donations from companies and individual citizens helped in this effort and within one month eighty-nine percent of the factory was up and running in the buildings that had been spared. Grateful employees worked hard to restore the company. Error rates fell to less than two percent, and a year later there were plans to build a new two-story, 600,000-square-foot textile factory. There was no appreciable loss of market share.

This remarkable CEO who could have easily taken the fire insurance money to finance a leisurely retirement, refused to turn his back on his customers, his employees, his stockholders, and the town that would have been overwhelmed by the permanent loss of his mills.

This fire and its aftermath were important events in the community of Lowell. Buffeted by a recent national economic recession, the city had its share of increased social problems, including violent crime. The loss of the mills would have increased unemployment and further diminished the city's revenue base and might well have jeopardized the city's hard-fought attempts at recovery. Instead of possible chaos, the city and its mills continue to grow two years later, after that fateful winter's day.

The importance of business for the community of Lowell has its counterparts in cities and towns throughout the nation. Profitability strengthens community and decreases the possibility of violence.

As we noted earlier, profitability also provides companies with the resources to be socially responsive to other community needs. Here are some examples.

Several companies have chosen health care as an area of corporate concern. Nationally, Service Merchandise raises money for muscular dystrophy; Enesco, a giftware industry, supports Easter Seals; and the RE/MAX real estate employees secure funds for the Children's Miracle Network, a program for hospitalized children. On a more local level, the Revenna Bank in Ohio supports cerebral palsy victims.

Other companies have focused on the environment. Body Shop International in England produces a range of personal care products that emphasize traditional and native methods of cleansing and softening the skin and hair, as well as environmental issues like minimal packaging and recycling efforts. Stoneyfield Farms, a yogurt manufacturer in New Hampshire, helped preserve several small farms by assisting them in growing organically healthy food products. Similarly, the Wisconsin Electric Power Company, based in Milwaukee, has been involved in several Nature Conservancy Projects statewide. Still other companies such as Coca-Cola and MCI have channeled considerable sums of money for a variety of educational endeavors.

All of these corporate initiatives in their own way contribute to strengthened neighborhoods and greatly reduced crime.

*Family-Friendly Programs.* The emergence of the postindustrial state has changed the nature of the work force, which is now composed of increasing numbers of two-wage-earner couples and single working parents. These parents are hard-pressed to meet responsibilities to both work and family, and business has become increasingly responsive to this need with a number of creative solutions that strengthen families at no loss to productivity. Businesses institute these programs for sound bottom-line reasons: increased productivity, less turnover, less absenteeism, and improved employee loyalty and morale. An important, but again often overlooked, benefit from these programs is their powerful effect on containing possible violent crime in families and communities. Each of these family-friendly programs fosters caring attachments among family and neighbors, and, as we have seen, caring attachments and meaningful human contact preclude violence.

Family-friendly programs are many and varied, but can be divided into two general groupings: work hour arrangements so that parents have more time to be with children, and direct programs that support needed family services.

In the first group, companies have several different approaches. Included are flex-time hours, job sharing, part-time positions, working at home, or compressed work weeks (e.g., working four ten-hour days). Each of these initiatives allows the parent(s) to shape his or her work week and family responsibilities so that both sets of responsibilities are met with less life stress.

Supporting these work hour choices are an additional array of company benefits to support employee dependents: childbirth leave, paid maternity leave, a phase-back period to the worksite for new mothers, adoption aid, sick days that can be utilized when children are ill, dependent care monies for children and elder-services are some of the more common initiatives.

Eli Lilly, Hewlett Packard, IBM, Johnson and Johnson, and Xerox Corporation have been consistent leaders in the area of family-friendly programs and their numbers are increasing. *Business Week* and *Working Mother* magazines publish surveys of family-friendly companies.

### Strengthening Community: Special Areas

The third approach by business to addressing the problems of violence in communities is to support specific programs that are designed to ameliorate the negative impact of specific sociological risk factors. Many businesses are again quietly engaged in such programs as part of their corporate mission. Here is a representative sample of some of these initiatives that address differing risk factors.

*The Permanent Underclass.* Several companies have created programs that directly address issues of poverty. Northwest Airlines,

Target department stores, and Honeywell Manufacturing support Habitat for Humanity International. The Habitat program, begun over twenty years ago, has provided housing for over fifty thousand people worldwide. The Adidas footwear industry has become a city-wide corporate sponsor of junior varsity league teams in the boroughs of New York City on the assumption that sports keep students in school. The Honda automobile company has created the Eagle Rock program in Colorado, which teaches individuals basic skills for life and work, and The Body Shop has started projects in New York City to employ the homeless and youth-at-risk in Baltimore, Maryland.

*Domestic Battering.* The Polaroid Corporation has been exemplary in these matters. Not only have they supported their own employee victims of domestic violence, but they have worked with community agencies to address this need at the neighborhood level. In Quincy, Massachusetts, the company worked with police, corrections, the courts, social service agencies, and shelters for battered women to create a model integrated program to address this need. In a state where domestic violence results on average in one death every ten days, there has not been one death from spousal abuse in this city since the day that the program was fielded. Similarly, the Healthtex Corporation, a leading manufacturer of children's wear, has donated some of its children's garments to a shelter for battered women and children.

*The Media.* A number of corporations address the issue of violence in the media by presenting programs in the arts totally unrelated to violence. The Aventa Corporation, a financial company, sponsored a museum exhibit at the Philadelphia Museum of Art. Thompson/RCA, an electronics firm, sponsors performing arts programs for high schools in Indianapolis. The Group W/Westinghouse Broadcasting Corporation sponsored a year-long series of media programs on alternatives to violence, while the Blue Fish Clothing Company of New Jersey has sponsored a series of hands-on art workshops for inner-city schools in Philadelphia.

In each of these examples, companies have directly addressed sociological risk factors to strengthen community in ways that normal business activity might not. There is still one more area where business can provide important leadership to reduce the risk of harm to customers and employees—the area of violence in the workplace.

*Violence in the Workplace*

There are several effective strategies to contain or minimize the risk of such violence, and some of the more common ones are presented in Table 1.

TABLE 1

**Addressing Violence in the Workplace: A Checklist:**

☐ *Securing the Facility*
    Controlled Access
    Ongoing Surveillance

☐ *Warning Signs of Potential Loss of Control*
    Appearance
    Behavior

☐ *System of Self-Defense*

☐ *Corporate Policy*
    Pre-Employment Screening
    Employee Assistance Program
    Threat Team
    Buddy System

*Securing the Facility.* The first risk-management strategy is to secure the physical plant of the facility from easy access to criminals. This is accomplished through controlling access and through ongoing surveillance.

Controlled access is preventing crime by environmental changes that enhance the probability of the assailant's being caught. Since most criminals depend on the element of surprise, when that is removed, criminals are likely to move on to other targets. Controlled access permits only those with legitimate reasons to be in the building to gain entry.

Keeping shrubs around the building low and at a distance from the building, having adequate lighting, keeping windows clear for visibility both inside and outside, and having an adequate number of employees on-site are all associated with less crime and violence.

Access is further controlled by the use of appropriate locks, bolts, electronic admissions systems, cameras, mirrors, and displayed television monitors. All of these suggest to the criminal that the chances of being recognized and apprehended outweigh the risks of the possible criminal behavior.

Ongoing surveillance is the second step in securing the facility. Once legitimate employees and customers have gained access, the company wants to be sure that intruders do not enter during the course of business hours. The cameras, mirrors, and electronics that we have discussed above are also helpful in ongoing surveillance. To these should be added some system of photo identification for regular employees and special passes for visitors. All visitors to the facility should readily stand out. It is also helpful to develop an emergency notification system with call buttons under desks or some sort of coded message for use in any public address system within the building.

*Early Warning Signs.* All employees and managers will want to learn the early warning signs of impending loss of control and practice how to summon assistance immediately. Early warning signs may be noticed both in appearance and behavior: a general state of dishevelment or disorganization, tense facial expressions, glazed eyes (usually due to substance abuse), and the wearing of sunglasses indoors (possible signs of paranoid thinking or substance abuse) serve as potential warning signs to observers.

Similarly, behavioral signs of severe agitation such as pacing, pounding, stammering; verbal threats toward specific persons; threats of weapons; and obvious signs of substance abuse, such as alcohol on the person's breath should again alert employees to the possibility of tenuous control and impending aggression. The presence of these signs does not necessarily mean that violence will follow, but these signs do bear watching. In general, the greater the number of signs present at any one time, the greater the likelihood of loss of control. Employees should be alert to the possible need to summon help.

*System of Self-Defense.* Companies whose employees deal directly with the public in frequent cash transactions are especially at risk for violence. Taxi cab companies, liquor stores, gas stations, hotels/motels, package express companies, healthcare workers, and others may need to be specially trained in some system of self-defense. This system should be chosen by the company and should adhere to any federal, state, or local policies. The training should be provided at company expense by qualified instructors to avoid any undue liability issues.

*Corporate Policy*. The risk of violence in the workplace can also be lessened by direct corporate policy in the areas of company regulations, screening procedures during hiring, the utilization of the employees assistance program (EAP), and the fielding of a threat team.

Corporate policies on matters associated with violence should be clearly stated in writing. There should be zero tolerance for weapons on company property whether at work stations or in lockers. Similarly, there should be zero tolerance for the presence of alcohol or drugs on company property. Employees should not drink alcohol two hours before work nor drink alcohol at company functions or during meal times and coffee breaks. To permit otherwise is to court violence unnecessarily.

Employment screening is an effective method of reducing the risk of violence from people for whom the company may be held responsible. Written permission should be obtained from the applicant, and work histories, credit histories, past histories of any felonies, and letters of reference should be examined in detail, but in accordance with any state or local regulations governing these matters. Interviewing notes should be written and kept in personnel files, should the need for such information arise later on.

Although adequate screening can help to rule out problematic employees before they are hired, employee assistance programs can provide training for current employees that further reduces the risk of aggression. Programs for treating substance abuse should be available, but so also should be workshops in verbal conflict resolution, advance technical training, and programs for managers in disciplining, laying off, or terminating employees in humane ways. Attention to these matters avoids unnecessary violent outbursts.

Corporate policy should also dictate the need for a threat team. Companies should have zero tolerance for threats of any type toward anyone. The threat team should be composed of company legal counsel, human resources, and security. This group evaluates all threats by interviewing the recipient of the threat, any employee who may have witnessed the threat, and the person who made the threat. If the individual who made the threat is an employee, all hiring materials should be reviewed as well as any indication of current problems and severe life stress. This information gathering is done in accordance with law, and the threat team, based on its findings, then makes appropriate recommendations for penalties to management. The very fact of a threat team provides a strong nonverbal message to the workforce that such behavior is unacceptable.

The threat team may prove especially helpful to employees who are victims of domestic battering. Such employees should be encouraged to share this information with the company threat team without fear of any corporate reprisal. The threat team can then plan appropriate strategies in house to address the matter should the assailant appear at the worksite. The threat team may also work out appropriate responses with the local police.

Finally, informal corporate policy should foster a buddy system for any high-risk areas on grounds. The most common of these include stairwells, bathrooms, elevators, and parking lots. Employees should be encouraged to pay special attention to these high-risk areas and to go in pairs, if necessary.

These steps for safety are far less expensive than one lawsuit successfully brought against a company, and, along with other socially responsible general business practices, represent a significant contribution by business toward reducing the national increase in violent crime. Owners, managers, employees, customers, and stockholders as well as ordinary citizens can encourage these forms of corporate helpfulness.

### Government

The institution of a freely elected government at all levels exists to serve the common good and to provide for the welfare of its citizens by ensuring that they have a reasonable voice in accessing the resources of society needed for everyday life. As with business, government may provide programs to strengthen community as well as to develop specific programs for the various sociological risk factors for violence. This twofold approach, in concert with the initiatives from business and our other societal institutions, further lessens anomie and holds the various risk factors for violent crime to a minimum.

There are hundreds, if not thousands, of programs sponsored by various government agencies, and we can only highlight some of these efforts here. Readers who are employees of federal and state agencies may have opportunities to affect programming at that level. For most, efforts to influence government policy are done at the local, municipal level and in the neighborhoods themselves. These grass roots approaches can be very effective in shaping immediate community needs as well as national policy at a later date. For example, many people agree that the country needs national educational standards to educate our youth for the postindustrial state. While most of us cannot affect national public policy directly, we can start in our own neighborhoods with our own local schools and begin to develop needed standards at home.

Similarly, in our own neighborhoods we can begin to address the problems of violent crime in very simple ways. We can be alert for strangers, and watch out for one another. In like manner, we can begin to think about the government initiatives that we are about to review and to consider how these could be modified and fielded at the community level.

### Strengthening Community: Basic Approaches

In an era of international economic competition, the government can protect its citizens and strengthen community in general with policies in four possible areas: protectionism, education and training, public works, and tax policies.

Protectionism refers to restriction imposed by the government on trading with other countries so that they do not have an unfair competitive advantage against our own goods and services. Programs in education and training can reeducate our citizens to be knowledgeable about the latest technological advances so that they remain competitive at home and abroad, when compared to the work forces of other countries. Public works programs are a third intervention that can strengthen community by providing employment for citizens so that locally needed problems are solved, such as having local bridges repaired. Finally, the government can strengthen community by tax policies that transfer income to those in need.

These interventions, if they are employed at various levels of government, need to be thought through adequately. The goal is to strengthen business and communities without disturbing effective business practices and general beneficial principles of free trade among countries. We need our citizens to be members of the postindustrial state and not the permanent underclass. Several observers of the government/business interface (Derber, 1991; Gordon, 1996; Kapstein, 1996; Kortner, 1995; Thurow, 1996) have raised a number of thoughtful approaches to these matters for public discussion and the reader may want to examine these suggestions in greater depth.

There is also the need for public discussion, informed debate, and the emergence of sound public policy on issues that are related to the possible risk factors for violence. These discussions are the responsibility of each of us in our common efforts to reduce violence and strengthen community. Topics include, among others: corporate welfare, campaign financing reform, term limits for office holders, standards for education, gun control, substance abuse, services for victims of untreated PTSD, and privacy issues in technology.

For example, many companies and businesses are provided subsidies and tax breaks that lessen the costs of daily business, but there is no real need for these government benefits. This is known as "corporate welfare." Such benefits may be found in agriculture, energy, timber, manufacturing, and the like, and cost the federal government about one hundred and fifty billion dollars each year. It is in the interest of the country to curtail these unneeded payments, but the process is complicated by political donations from these companies to the country's elected representatives.

The vibrancy of a democracy depends upon the true independence of its legislative bodies to consider the requests and needs of all of its citizens. Solutions need to be determined and compromises need to be reached, but the process should be inherently open to a review of each issue solely on its merits. Theoretically, any citizen should be able to seek elective office, and, if elected, to enter into legislative deliberation with an open mind and a responsivity to the citizens whom the person represents.

However, the process of running for office in our country has become so expensive that those of great wealth can exert undue influence on our elected representatives by contributing vast sums of money to the legislators' re-election campaigns. Such an inherent structural tension exists between business and government. Businesses hire lobbyists whose task is to influence legislation on behalf of business interests and to obtain the government subsidies and tax benefits that we have noted. However, the desires of business (for example, the easing of environmental regulations) may not always be in the best common interest, but the goal of the lobbyist is to prevail in persuading legislators to act in the best interests of business.

One possible solution to this problem of corporate welfare might be the designation of an independent review commission to function as the military-base closure commission did a few years ago. When the Communist threat declined in recent years, the country had more military bases than it needed. Since these bases were located in many states, and provided large payrolls to local states and communities, legislators were reluctant to close bases in their own states. To address the problem, the base closure commission was asked to review these installations, and to make recommendations of which bases should be closed. Congress then had to vote in the affirmative or the negative for the entire list.

A similar process could be used to develop guidelines and limits for all corporate subsidies. A commission would be appointed to devise strategies to curb the inherent structural tension by all business interest groups. Congress would then vote to accept or reject the package. If passed, the new guidelines would have similar applicability at the state and municipal levels.

Discussions such as this are needed for the other topics that we have noted, since these issues and their solutions directly relate to our staying competitive internationally, reducing the size of the permanent underclass, and directly addressing the factors associated with the increased levels of violent crime, which we have documented. The discussion of these matters could begin with neighbors visiting with each other in community meetings at the local school, in the local media as well as in the traditional national, state, and municipal forums for legislative debate. To the extent that individuals participate in the shaping of these policies, they will experience shared values around a common task and anomie will be lessened.

In the interim, government at all levels can begin to formulate more focused policies that strengthen families and, thus, communities. For example, government can work to foster employee corporate ownership in this era of downsizing, to promote employee stock options through tax incentives, to strengthen savings, pension, and retirement plans in the face of dwindling Social Security resources. Many of these initiatives can be addressed locally and in the longer term neighborhoods are strengthened by such programs.

## Strengthening Community: Special Areas

As was the case with the business community, various government agencies also have begun programs specifically to address the sociological risk factors that are associated with high levels of violent crime.

*The Permanent Underclass.* Some state and local governments have taken the initiative in creating business enterprise zones in less affluent neighborhoods such as those in areas of Atlanta and Detroit. Reduced taxes and the provision of city services such as roads and sewerage linkups make it possible for businesses to hire local residents and to stimulate the local economy through their payrolls.

Government at all levels can foster the education and training of individuals so that they acquire the skills that keep them above the poverty level. Government can provide tax incentives for companies to do this, or they can find programs directly or in cooperation with national charitable foundations. For example, the W. K. Kellogg Foundation has worked with local governments and neighborhood groups to fund a variety of programs for at-risk youth that include mentoring, job training, and church-based support groups. Similarly, the Ford Foundation has fielded an initiative with local governments to reconnect absent fathers with their children by providing needed job training and assistance in obtaining work. The school system in Hartford, Connecticut, is an example of direct government involvement in its own right as it seeks to avoid discrimination in education in providing a quality education to each of its young people. Currently under discussion as possible alternatives are charter schools, magnet schools, school choice, or some form of a voucher system.

There are many other examples of citizen and government involvement that creatively address the issue of the permanent underclass. Eighteen years ago, Dorothy Stoneman decided to help young people gain skills and enhance their self-esteem. Her program, Youthbuild USA, helps teenagers build housing for homeless or low-income citizens and provides them with opportunities for alternative academic and leadership skills. Youthbuild now has one hundred programs in thirty-four states.

Government and the private sector in Louisville, Kentucky, have formed a program to provide students with summer jobs. The students agree to study hard for good grades during the academic year and are promised summer employment in return for their efforts.

With better response times, better building codes, and fire detectors, the fire departments in Miami and Charlotte now use some of their time to clear baseball diamonds, coach students, and provide services for the homeless. The police department in Casselberry, Florida, has a call-back service for the many elderly in the community that they serve. An automated phone service rings elderly residents. If there is no response, the police visit to find out whether the person needs assistance.

Vanderbilt University created a program to meet the needs of aggressive children at high risk to become violent adults. Teachers in Seattle, Washington, Durham, North Carolina, Nashville, Tennessee, and rural Pennsylvania were trained to help the angry children learn to get along with others and share things. There were clear rules and time-outs for aggressive outbursts. Aggressive children in the fourth grade in each of these test cities were compared to aggressive children who were not in the fast-track program. At the end of the program, forty percent of the no-treatment comparison group were in special education classes whereas only twenty-three percent of the intervention group had been assigned to special classes.

*Domestic Abuse.* Since we have seen how an abused child very often becomes an abusing adult (Widom, 1992), it is important for local government to add to its resources for addressing this important national need. Local governments can be helpful in creating more shelters for battered women and their children, to strengthen local laws that increase the penalties for violating restraining orders, and to foster more active policing of this problem. For example, in this latter case, the police department in Minneapolis, found that the battering of spousal victims ceased if the batterer was arrested rather than being ordered to leave the home for a few hours. Other states in the Midwest have found that coupling the arrest with prosecution by the police department rather than by the frightened spouse results in even greater reductions in subsequent episodes of battering. These approaches along with better risk management strategies for stopping batterers in the workplace can significantly reduce this risk factor. Violence need not breed violence when we have learned how to intervene successfully.

*Community Policing.* New and improved policing strategies appear to contribute, at least in part, to the declines in violent crime noted in chapter 1. These include longer prison sentences, a crackdown on illegal guns, gun buy-back plans, the interdiction of illegal drugs, and computerized targeting of high-crime areas. However, an equally important experiment in strengthening community is also taking place within the police community. Known as *community policing*, the goal is to remove officers from patrol cars and have them patrol neighborhoods on foot (or bicycles). The goal is for the officer to get to know the residents of the neighborhood so that trends in violent crime can be identified and solved quickly. This approach addresses several of the risk factors at once, such as substance abuse, domestic violence, hate-based crimes of discrimination, and criminal behavior associated with the permanent underclass. Many police departments nationwide are implementing this approach, and the results have been remarkable.

Consider some of its many examples. In Chicago, the police received a grant for one million dollars to apprehend the city's worst young offenders in gangs. Utilizing racketeering statutes, high-tech wiretaps and money laundering laws, they have been able to arrest thirty-nine gang leaders. Miami, Dallas, Los Angeles, and eleven other cities have received federal monies for similar programs.

In Phoenix, the police have begun neighborhood block watches, antigraffiti campaigns, and the education of children in the school system on safety and crime issues. In Philadelphia, the police meet with community groups to role-play mock arrests in order to avoid community backlashes later on. The Fort Worth police have trained hundreds of citizens for neighborhood patrols and have focused the attention of at-risk youth on recreational activities to keep them from joining gangs. On the theory that criminals commit fewer serious offenses as well as serious crimes, police in New York City have begun enforcing laws on smoking marijuana, shoplifting, and evading subway fares in a crackdown on so-called quality-of-life issues, and it has resulted in a dramatic decrease in serious crime citywide as criminals are stopped for the less serious offenses. Eugene, Oregon, has acquired a state-of-the-art motor vehicle to apprehend drunken drivers.

These mutual efforts are examples of successful interventions to take back the streets from violent criminals. The sense of community is strengthened in the process.

*Youth Violence.* Most citizens acknowledge that we have a serious problem with youth crime. Less well known is that there are several solutions known to be effective in preventing such violence.

Table 2 outlines these basic approaches. In general, the younger the child is when provided with these helpful interventions, the greater the likelihood of preventing subsequent violence.

TABLE 2

**Approaches for Preventing Youth Violence:**

*Academics*
> Verbal Conflict Resolution
> Vocational Education

*Caring Attachments*
> Mentors
> Tutors
> Big Brother/Big Sister
> Foster Parents
> Foster Grandparents

*Policing*
> Curfew
> Teen Courts
> Truancy Patrols

*Social Learning*
> Summer Jobs
> Recreation Programs

*Treatment Interventions*
> Child Abuse
> Substance Abuse

An inspection of the items in Table 2 suggests that there are important roles for each of five major institutions in addressing these needs, including those efforts by government. We have seen how business has fielded some helpful initiatives in the areas of academics and social learning, and government has an equally important role. Government may address academics through its school system as we shall see in the next chapter, but it may also provide the leadership in other areas of need.

Local government, in conjunction with the business sector, private foundations, and interested neighborhoods, can field big brother/big sister programs, and foster parent and foster-grandparent programs. These approaches build caring attachments to isolated youth, and provide tutors, mentors, and role models in acquiring basic academic and social skills. Local governments are in a unique position to sponsor recreational programs and to encourage companies to create summer jobs for students.

Similarly, the municipal community can be of assistance on other matters. Truancy patrols are helpful. Many of our large cities have also found teen curfews to reduce crime and violence, and in twenty-four states 185 teen courts pass judgments on their peers. This last approach has a twofold benefit: peers pass sentences on peers and, thus, adults are not blamed for being unfair; and young people are learning about the law and civic responsibility.

Finally, government resources could be directed to provide start-up monies and ongoing funding for programs that address child abuse and substance abuse, factors that at times are both associated with violence. These sociological risk factors greatly enhance the possibility of membership in the permanent underclass and a life of violent crime. Early intervention programs have been shown to be effective, and at present, they are seriously underfunded for those in need of such programs.

### Addressing the Aftermath of Violence in the Workplace

In conjunction with business, the government has been active in addressing the issues of violence in the workplace, particularly through the federal Occupational Safety and Health Administration (OSHA). OSHA has been a consistent advocate for reducing the risk for violence in the workplace.

Since some episodes of violence in the workplace will occur even with risk management strategies in place, a state governmental agency, the Massachusetts Department of Mental Health, has fielded an initiative to treat the psychological aftermath of violent episodes in which patients assault employees. Not only has the program provided helpful support for staff victims, but it is also associated with *sharp reductions in violence*. These findings have been replicated and the program may be adapted to a variety of settings, including schools, colleges, corrections, and health care and industrial settings.

*The Assaulted Staff Action Program (ASAP)* (Flannery, 1995) is a voluntary, systemwide, peer-help, crisis intervention debriefing program for staff who are assaulted by patients in hospital and community-based settings. When an assault occurs, the ASAP team member is summoned by beeper to the employee victim's worksite, and debriefs the employee, if the employee accepts the service. Additional services include debriefings of entire wards in cases of extreme violence to the whole patient and staff community, a staff victims' support group, and family counseling for the employee victim's family, where indicated. In their interventions, ASAP team members seek to restore or instill the skills of stress-resistant persons by helping employee victims restore a sense of personal mastery, reestablish their network of caring attachments, and to make meaning of the violent episode.

The ASAP program believes that employees are worthy of compassionate care, that talking in the short term helps and prevents the onset of PTSD over the longer term, and that receiving help from peers at the same risk of assault is more supportive than counseling by others not at the same risk. The ASAP philosophy and the provision of its services is a conscious attempt to strengthen community by creating a culture of compassion and caring attachments.

To date, there are ten ASAP programs with one hundred and fifty ASAP team members who have provided over one-hundred-and-twenty-five-thousand hours of volunteer service to their health care worksites. ASAP has provided highly regarded support services in the aftermath of violent episodes and in the four programs that have been on-line for a year, there have been reductions in the level of violence in *each* facility that exceed forty percent.

The capacity for ASAP to strengthen the sense of community as well as enhance its safety suggests the potential helpfulness of this government-sponsored approach for the other worksite settings noted earlier.

This chapter has outlined a number of effective approaches in business and government that address our national public health problem with violence. These programs reduce and contain violent crime by addressing both the sociological risk factors for violence and the need to strengthen community in an age of anomie. These changes are being accomplished by ordinary citizens and groups of citizens

# 6

# RESTORING COMMUNITY: FAMILY, SCHOOL, AND RELIGION

*Friendship is a sheltering tree.*
— Samuel Taylor Coleridge

*Look after him; and if you spend any more,*
*I shall repay you on my way back.*
— Luke 10:35

*Dateline: Ponchatoula, Louisiana. March 8, 1995.*

Click. . . . Click. . . . Click. . . . One frame every three seconds.
"I did not see her, I saw the demon."
The beeping of the respirator . . .
A family devoted to public service. One United States Congressman. One state governor. One state's attorney general who opposed gun control.
The Federal Bureau of Investigation agent had arrived late in the afternoon with warrants for his daughter's arrest. As a courtesy, they would allow him to speak with her first and they returned to their cars to wait. When she returned home from an amusement park at eleven-thirty in the evening, the father enfolded his daughter on the front porch of the large gray home and instructed her to be brave and to remember that she had the right to remain silent. The agents then arrested the daughter of this circuit court judge.
She had been a child of promise in her buoyant early youth—until age fourteen when that growth was stunted three times by deaths. The first, the suicide of her best friend. The second, the loss of another good friend in a car accident. The third, the death of her grandfather, the congressman. Struggles with depression, suicidal thinking, drugs, and lying followed.
On March 6, the eighteen-year-old daughter and her eighteen-year-old boyfriend decided to drive from their midwest homes south to a concert and then on to Florida. Death had also crossed the boyfriend's

life when his alcoholic father committed suicide. The boy was thirteen years of age. Later, the boy dropped out of high school and became involved with drugs, but this was in the past. The couple packed the car with their belongings and with a belonging that was not theirs, the judge's thirty-eight caliber revolver.

On March 7, the owner of a local cotton gin sat at his desk in Hernando, Mississippi. For over thirty years he and his wife had run this business, reared a family and found time to make frequent church mission trips to Central America. When his office door opened unexpectedly, he looked up and was shot dead in the face at point blank range by the judge's gun allegedly in the hands of the boyfriend.

On March 8, the slender mother of three tidied the house, admired her new diamond wedding ring, a gift from her husband on their twentieth wedding anniversary, and left for work as the all-night counter clerk at the Ponchatoula convenience store.

Click. A young woman with a candy bar approaches the counter. Click. The convenience store clerk approaches the register. Click. The older woman recoils from the force of the gunshot to her neck by the younger woman, again with the judge's gun. Click. The assailant returns to the register for money. The security camera clicked again with its permanent record.

The beeping of the respirator marked the beginning of a lifetime of quadriplegia for the convenience store clerk. She refused to see her children and lived in self-imposed darkness for five months. She had prayed daily for death until one day the respirator sounded its alarm and her pulse fell to zero. Her prayers for death stopped lest her wish come true.

One severed spinal cord. Several severed dreams. An equal number of broken hearts in three states.

*I did not see her, I saw the demon,* recalled the young female assailant.

Death, depression, and darkness continued to exact their toll.

The respirator beeped in the darkness.

Here we have yet another example of violence and human suffering, an illustration of one of every parent's worst fears. In two sleepy rural towns, the lives of four families were permanently shattered. Did family, schooling, and religion fail these two young people, or were these supports overridden by substance abuse, available weapons, mental illness, or a culture of personal entitlement with no sense of responsibility toward others?

These matters await adjudication in the courts, but the very questions raised by this case point to the importance of these three societal institutions in containing and curtailing violence, and they are examined in this final chapter. Family, school, and religion are the basic foundations in society that prevent such tragedies from occurring and that sustain the victims and their loved ones when such tragedies occur.

These three institutions also sustain parents and facilitate childrearing to ensure the growth of a new generation of morally responsible and socially productive young citizens who are not disposed to violent crime.

As in the previous chapter, we want to examine approaches that both strengthen the sense of community and mitigate specific sociological risk factors, since both are needed for effective long-term control of violence. As with business and government, we will want to examine both the familiar and the new. The recent sharp increases in youth crime serve as a reminder of the importance of being sure that the familiar have been addressed and not overlooked in an age of time-pressured anomie, while the new may have helpful additions for us to consider.

Before we begin to examine how these institutions can strengthen community, we want to draw our attention to a frequently absent community voice: fathers. We have noted in our earlier review of the current findings on crime as well as in our study of criminals over a fifty-year period, that broken homes and inadequate parenting were commonly associated with delinquent or adult criminal offspring. Most often that missing family resource is the father.

Sociologist David Popenoe (1996) has recently added an important body of evidence that may help us understand part of the cause for our current high rates of crime. Because of deaths, nonmarital births, and high divorce rates, the sociological data reveal a sharp drop in the presence of fathers in the home during the 1960s to the present, the same years in which we have noted the sharp increases in crime.

Fathers play an important role in child development, a role different from and complementary to that of mothers. Fathers add protection and discipline to the family unit, and rough-and-tumble play that fosters independent and cooperative behavior. They are also an important moral voice, and both fathers and children suffer from its absence. When these bonds are disrupted, children are at higher risk for economic loss, academic problems, unemployment, subsequent child abuse, and criminal and violent behavior (Popenoe, 1996).

Fathers themselves are at risk for impaired physical and mental health, a loss of the sense of well-being, more criminal behavior, more violence, and premature death (Flannery, 1992, 1994). Society, especially its children, is paying an unacceptable price, and the suggestions presented in this chapter are for both fathers and mothers.

In this chapter, we also continue our inquiry into how to strengthen community in the face of the various risk factors that may lead to violent crime. In examining the roles of family, school, and religion, our focus again will be on what individual citizens can accomplish at the neighborhood level, either singly or in small groups.

A suggestion as we begin: while it is true that we need to curb the violence in our society, it is also true that many of us feel overwhelmed by the stress of life, and any process of change seems difficult to consider. To avoid this sense of overload, it may be helpful to read the chapter fully and then to choose one of these three institutions in which you commit your efforts in reducing violence. Choose one soluble problem within that institutional context. Choose a less complicated problem to begin with so that you can experience some success. In this way, there will be one less problem to solve and you will feel motivated to continue. This approach of solving problems in small, manageable steps will help with the sense of feeling overburdened or overwhelmed.

# Families

## *Strengthening Community: Basic Approaches*

The family is our basic societal institution for rearing children to be contributing members of society at work, in their own families, and in their neighborhoods. Childrearing is never an easy task in any age and it is more complicated in our own because of the postindustrial shift, values that emphasize self rather than others, and increased levels of violence in society. Rearing children who will not be perpetrators of violence, and who will not themselves be victims of needless violence requires constant vigilance by parents over a period of several years.

Yet, two-career families, working women, and single parents are frequently short of time and long on responsibilities. Work, day care, summer camp, dance recitals, aging parents fill already overcrowded days. Consider the many sacrifices that you must make to accomplish these goals. What to do? Where to begin? How much time to spend on each task?

Because of the importance of parents' being at their best in tasks with their children, this section on families reviews basic issues and solutions facing parents as persons in their own right, and then explores specific childrearing issues in today's age. The family strengthens community and neighborhood when the family fosters mastery, caring attachments, and a meaningful purpose in life for each of its members. The suggestions presented herein are directed toward these goals.

### Empowering Parents

Parents today face a number of common problems that may impair their quality of life and make the task of childrearing more difficult. In fact, some of these problems may place that parent and child in harm's way. Included in this list of postindustrial complications are increased life stress, competing value systems for oneself and one's children, parental substance abuse, domestic violence, adequate day care, and parental rights. Resolving these matters first provides parents with more time and energy for their children.

*Increased Life Stress.* The shifts in the postindustrial state that have resulted in increased competition and increased time-urgency leave many parents overwhelmed and tired out. Since they realize that stressful life problems are better solved when they are at their best, many of today's parents make time to include the basic stress management approach of stress-resistant persons. They understand that the energy invested in a stress management approach yields rich dividends in terms of sustained health and a clarity of mind that saves time in other areas of their lives.

Making time for relaxation periods each day and aerobic exercise each week are two approaches that are powerful means for reducing the physiology of stress, regardless of the particular problems that a person may be facing. Reasonable nutrition and time with other caring persons for support and companionship are similarly helpful in reducing life stress. Taken together, these steps restore energy and provide time to think more clearly about one's daily routine in general, and the task of rearing children in particular.

*Competing Values.* The postindustrial state has also left parents with two fundamentally different and competing value systems.

Choosing the values for one's life and the values to teach one's children are not easy tasks. We have seen how the present primary cultural values of personal entitlement, material acquisition and instant gratification are leading to a callous society, with violence and other lesser forms of harshness. Is the cultural emphasis on power, success, fame, and material acquisition worth the price? The pursuit of these objectives requires a great deal of time and intense competitive pressure with resultant loss of energy and less time for personal and family pursuits. Even successful attainment of these goals frequently leaves the person bored, socially isolated, and lonely. Values that emphasize honesty, trust, responsibility for self and others appear to be better values for oneself and for one's children, and are needed in today's society. However, these are not the major values in society and adhering to them and teaching them to one's children is difficult in the face of the postindustrial cultural pressure. Parents may want to consider the best that each system has to offer (e.g., balancing reasonable material gain with concern for the welfare of others).

*Substance Abuse.* Parenting is difficult enough without complicating the process further with drugs or alcohol. Substance abuse is inordinately expensive, consumes many hours spent in feeding the addiction, precludes learning better ways to cope, and badly damages caring attachments to children. While heroin, crack/cocaine, and marijuana are frequent parental drugs of choice, alcohol is the most common offender.

Alcoholism is present when one's drinking causes trouble. It is not defined by the type of alcohol consumed or the amount that the person consumes. If one's drinking gets one into trouble, then one is drinking alcoholically. Trouble includes problems with one's boss, spouse, children, physical and mental health, or with the law. In our clinics we often ask a person four questions about alcohol: (1) Do you need an eye-opener? (2) Do you get angry when people discuss alcohol? (3) Has anyone ever told you to cut back on your consumption? (4) Do you feel guilty?

An answer of yes to two or more of these questions indicates problems with alcohol abuse. There are good treatments for both drug and alcohol abuse, and parents may wish to avail themselves of these opportunities to free themselves from this unnecessary life stress.

*Domestic Violence.* In a similar way, neither parents nor children deserve to be victims of violence. Nor is this violence more tolerable if the children are only witnesses to the violence. We should note that one can be psychologically traumatized equally by being a victim or by witnessing violent acts happening to others.

If one is a victim of spousal violence, there is help and there is no embarrassment in seeking it. Many police departments now have domestic violence units, and officers in many states are now required to arrest batterers. Many communities have shelters for battered women that provide safety and protection, and where children may accompany their mothers. Emergency rooms of hospitals, mental health counselors, family attorneys, and the clergy are all possible resources with which to begin.

If one is a single parent who is feeling overwhelmed and begins to abuse her children, parental abuse hotlines, mental health counselors, clergy, other parents, and other friends or relatives can be helpful in assisting that parent to gather needed support as well as better training in the parenting skills needed to solve problems in nonviolent ways.

Hawaii has an exemplary program in this regard. Hawaii Healthy Start is a social service program that screens all new mothers at the birth of their children. In particular, the staff is looking for mothers who are overwhelmed due to domestic violence, substance abuse, no prenatal care, or an attempted abortion of the new child. A family helper is assigned to the parent for five years. During this time, the parent has a support network and is taught how to reward and punish children safely, how to stimulate a child's curiosity, and the like. This program has reported sharp reductions in subsequent child abuse and there are now two hundred similar programs in thirty states.

The principle for success is clear: if one is feeling overwhelmed and abusive, there are many resources for support and help in learning parenting skills. Some abused parents believe that they cannot change, but the experience of those of us who counsel in a variety of settings is that this perception is inaccurate.

*Day Care.* Adequate day care is another important issue for today's parents and can be a source of great concern for parents. Parental work responsibilities frequently entail placing children in day care, and parents understandably want the best placement for their children. Some day care is provided by businesses for their employees, some by private agencies, some by public agencies, and some by extended families. Sometimes, groups of parents band together and rotate childrearing responsibilities when other alternatives are not available.

Recent findings by the National Institute of Child Health and Human Development have provided some encouraging results. This ten-site longitudinal study of 1,300 children has found no apparent negative effects on the development of caring attachments to parents in the first fifteen months of life. Some disrupted attachments were found in mothers who were insensitive or unresponsive to their children and who were anxious or depressed, but these disruptions appeared to be more a function of the parent's make-up than the day care setting itself.

While this is encouraging, it is still true that studies of day care placement are new and evolving. Several studies suggest that good day care programs teach the child excellent cognitive skills, but that social skills and feelings need to be strengthened by parents. A further concern is the lack of uniform standards for settings, staffing, and programmatic settings, but there are good day care settings and parents may want to leave time to assess several before making their choice.

*Parental Rights.* A final issue of common concern is the role of parental rights. In a society that emphasizes personal advancement and material gain, many of the responsibilities of parents have fallen to other social institutions such as the schools and government agencies, and many parents are not comfortable with what their children are being taught and how parents are being held responsible for the wayward behavior of their children.

A couple in Michigan was recently fined for their son's delinquent behavior. Another couple found that their third grade child was referred to counseling that they felt was not in the best interest of their child. Neither the school nor the courts would honor the parents' request to stop the counseling. Whereas states already have laws against parental child abuse and contributing to the delinquency of minors, about fifteen states have added additional parental liability laws to hold parents accountable for rearing their children properly.

Although some parents advocate for a congressional parental rights amendment that would protect the fundamental right of a parent to direct the upbringing of a child, these matters are difficult to legislate in practice. A more workable solution may lie in parents' reassertion of their moral authority over their children and working closely and cooperatively with schools and government agencies to find acceptable solutions to the children's needs.

This concerned interest by the adult community enhances caring attachments to children, provides a set of coherent moral guidelines, and, in time, strengthens community—with the risk for violence also declining.

## Issues in Childrearing

As we have noted, the goal of childrearing is to nurture children who become happy, productive, nonviolent adults. Creating reasonable mastery, caring attachments, and a meaningful purpose in life while avoiding as much as possible the sociological risk factors for violence are key factors in this process, and our discussion will focus on these domains. Since disrupted caring attachments are so fundamental in violence, we begin our discussion there.

*Caring Attachments.* Adequate caring attachments have several components and include spending time with the child, teaching the child how to trust others, instilling empathy, and developing adequate self-esteem.

Children find the presence of adults protective and comforting. Children need time to think, ask questions, try out solutions, ask for feedback and direction, and so forth. All of this takes adult time. Our public swimming pools, movie theaters, and public libraries are filled with children who are in need of more contact with their parents. For caring attachments to take root, children need time and attention in the physical presence of their parents.

Next, children need to learn how to trust. This is not guesswork or a feeling one has. Trust is composed of predictable behavior and similar values of concern for others. Predictable behavior means that what a person says that person will do is actually done. If the teacher promises to be in class each day at eight o'clock in the morning, and the teacher is there each day, then the teacher's behavior is predictable to the students. Since the world is a complicated place for all of us, we are given some leeway for making errors and not doing what we have said that we will do. As long as we have some reasonable explanation for these infrequent lapses, our behavior is considered predictable.

For this predictable behavior to be considered trustworthy, the second element of similar values of concern for others must be present in each party. Behavior that we can rely on must be motivated by honesty, support, and concern for one another. If someone values stealing and mayhem, one may be able to predict that person's deviant behavior, but that person would not be considered trust-worthy. Young children, particularly as they get older, can be taught this skill by assignments to observe the behavior and values of others and themselves, and then to report on the results.

A third component of developing caring attachments consists in teaching the child to have empathy and tolerance for others. Parents instill this skill by teaching children the correct labels for various feelings, by teaching the child when the child is experiencing these feelings and why these feelings are occurring, and then in going the next step and teaching the child when others have similar feelings and the reasons for why they are experiencing them. Feelings of joy, happiness, and excitement need to be learned and empathetically understood in others, along with the feelings of anger, guilt, sadness, and hurt. Children can practice empathy by considering how their pets, their siblings, their parents, and their friends may be feeling about a particular event. This process requires considerable feedback on the part of parents before it is mastered, but it is central to developing lifelong skills in understanding others and being tolerant of differences. Training in empathy early on decreases the probability of discrimination in later adult life.

A fourth component in caring attachments is accurate self-esteem. Adequate self-esteem is built on a true evaluation of a person's strengths and weaknesses, an adequate assessment of their responsibilities and rights. The events in a child's day are best evaluated individually. The child is told that he or she was good for putting away the toys and walking a brother across the street. The child is told that he or she was not good for stealing the extra cookies and not taking a bath. The child is told that he or she needs to develop better skills at riding the bicycle by means of more practice. This form of specifically referenced appraisal helps the child learn what the child does well and where more effort for growth is needed. Generalized statements without referents, such as "Tommy is a good boy," are of little help, and statements such as "you are just like your father" are not accurate and may confuse the child.

*Mastery.* While parents are developing and refining these attachment skills, they can also begin the work of developing reasonable mastery in their children. Children need to learn to shape the world to meet their needs, and are helped by parents who find a balance between encouraging independence and providing support during the learning periods. Sooner or later, the parent will not be present and the child will need to be able to cope alone. The scientific research indicates that children do best when attempting to do things by themselves with appropriate cognitive direction, emotional support, and guidance from the parents. This process of learning to master responsibility for self-care, care of property, and the care of others is greatly advanced if parents break each task into small manageable steps. The child's growth is further enhanced if the child develops the characteristics utilized by stress-resistant persons for managing stress and anger: good problem-solving skills, healthy lifestyle choices in diet and exercise, and the use of humor. The use of aerobic exercise also helps to reduce the potential for aggression, as recreation programs for at-risk youth across the country have demonstrated.

As children learn to master various specific tasks, they will also be able to develop a sense of personal responsibility. Businessperson Nancy Godfred (1995) has written a helpful book to teach children about responsibility. For example, when children begin to earn money, the family could have a citizen-of-the-household tax jar and a charity tax jar into which the child is expected to place a small percentage of the child's earnings. The child helps to decide how to spend the tax and charitable monies collected by all of the family's members. This simple procedure teaches children about civic responsibility as well as concern for the less fortunate. Her book contains many similar and helpful suggestions.

The child's sense of mastery is also enhanced with training in the more complex social and academic skills. Children need to learn to respect views and choices of others, to learn the basic social graces, to learn verbal conflict resolution skills for addressing the inevitable differences of opinion over life's many issues, and to have zero tolerance for weapons and for violence, except in cases of self-defense in the face of imminent harm. In these latter situations, children need to be taught when it is a matter of self-defense and how to deal with the bully.

Today's parents will also want to be active in overseeing the growth of their child's academic skills. Has the child learned the basics of English, math, and computer science? Is the child taking courses that will leave the child prepared for gainful employment in our postindustrial knowledge-based society? Does the child understand money matters, including banking and credit? Seeing that homework is done, participating closely with teachers, and being acquainted with the child's school friends are additional ways in which parents can enhance the mastery skills of their children.

Parents have developed some creative ways of teaching a variety of basic mastery skills. North Carolina and Georgia have mobilized local citizens in statewide efforts to combat the rise of teenage pregnancies. With public education and community outreach, the levels of teenage pregnancies have begun to decline. A hospital in New York City uses its waiting room for reading to children and teaching parenting skills to parents as the family waits for medical care. Seattle citizens address the anger in at-risk youth for violence by sponsoring the Seattle Summer Young Writer's Workshop. The program is teaching alternative ways to express anger without resorting to violence and has proven its value.

The National Task Force on African American Males sponsored by the Kellogg Foundation in 1992 developed several suggestions for black youth. Among other things, these included encouraging business development, requiring that school be year-round, developing a network of black-youth camps for recreation, and putting emphasis on education and the use of libraries. To address underage teenage alcohol abuse when driving, the citizens of thirty-four states have passed some sort of legislation that automatically suspends the license of a minor who is driving a car with any amount of alcohol in the minor's bloodstream. Their efforts in this regard have become a model for similar federal legislation.

*Meaningful Purpose.* A meaningful purpose in life is the third domain for parental consideration. The medical and scientific findings suggest that children are best served when they have a balance between reasonable ambition and a sense of responsibility toward others. The Declaration of Independence, the great religions of the world, and the characteristics of stress-resistant persons all emphasize concern for others as an integral part of developing a meaningful purpose in life. Values such as honesty, trustworthiness, being responsible, respecting the rights of others, and being concerned for the welfare of others appear to be in the long-term best interest of the child and of society.

Research shows us that children will learn these values best if they have clear definitions of what behaviors are acceptable and not acceptable, and what rewards or penalties should be expected. Children will learn these values correctly if discipline for unacceptable behaviors is consistent.

In addition to teaching these values directly, parents enhance their children's learning by role-modeling adult behavior that espouses these same values. Just as children learn to be aggressive through a social modeling learning process, they can also learn more pro-social behaviors. For additional values training, some parents have chosen to have their children attend religious observances or to enroll their child in a private school system that espouses values consistent with the parents' beliefs.

Being a volunteer is another excellent way to teach children compassion for others. A recent Gallup Poll for the Independent Sector, a coalition of volunteer groups in Metairie, Louisiana, indicated that about ninety million Americans volunteer about 19.5 billion hours of service for a dollar equivalent of $182 billion dollars. This is still a remarkable strength of our country; children should be encouraged to join in.

Children and teenagers may also be encouraged to volunteer to help the sick, the elderly, the homeless, and the like, or volunteer for causes such as protecting the environment or banning nuclear waste. Projects can be tapped for local need. For example, Mississippi has started a volunteer teacher corps, and recruits college graduates to volunteer to teach underprivileged for a year or two in return for a small stipend. The possibilities are endless and there are many local programs in need of such volunteer services to foster caring attachments and to strengthen the sense of community in local neighborhoods.

### Strengthening Community: Special Areas

To close our section on childrearing and violent behavior, we turn to three issues of special importance to parents: (1) substance abuse, (2) depression and suicidal thoughts that often accompany depression, and (3) the influence of the media.

*Substance Abuse.* Table 1 (following page) includes some of the more common warning signs of substance abuse. Teenage behavior is often inconsistent as the young adult tries new roles and new ways of coping, and some of the signs in Table 1 may be due to normal teen growth (for example, being depressed or not getting enough sleep). Some of the signs in Table 1 may also be due to medical illness, bereavement, and the side effects of prescribed medication, to name a few.

## TABLE 1

**Drug Abuse: Some Possible Warning Signs:**

| *Body Physiology* | *Feeling States* |
|---|---|
| Decreased Alertness | Depression |
| Loss of Appetite | Elation |
| Shallow Breathing | Hostility |
| Drowsiness | Irritability |
| Glazed Eyes | |
| Loss of Libido | *Behaviors* |
| Poor Motor Coordination | Appears Intoxicated |
| Dilated Pupils | Dark Glasses |
| Disturbed Sleep | Drug Paraphernalia |
| Slurred Speech | Long-Sleeve Shirts or Blouses (to hide needle marks) |

Thus, the signs in Table 1 are best considered as possible warnings, particularly if their appearance is sudden or occurs over a protracted period of time. If you are concerned, it is helpful to tell your child or adolescent of those concerns in a nonaccusatory manner, and to insist that these symptoms be evaluated by your family physician to rule our substance abuse or other serious illness. Parents will want to be particularly alert to alcohol abuse. Two in ten teenagers are addicted to alcohol and, since alcohol is usually the least expensive and most readily available drug, it is consumed more frequently. Violent deaths due to teenage drunk driving are at unacceptable levels; they devastate families and communities. If you find your child abusing drugs or alcohol, a variety of helpful treatment programs are available locally. Call the family physician or local hospital emergency room for information on where to begin.

*Depression.* Our country is also dealing with unacceptably high levels of adolescent depression and suicide, estimated by some accounts to be occurring nationally at the rate of one every fifty-nine minutes. Again, families and whole communities are impacted.

Table 2 presents some common signs of depression. As with the signs of possible drug abuse, these signs can be due to actual bereavement or some other major loss (for example one's job or one's home in a natural disaster), to untreated psychological trauma or PTSD, to serious medical illnesses, and, again, to the side effects of some medications. As with the signs of substance abuse in Table 1, the signs of possible depression in Table 2 are to be treated with equal seriousness. Ask the child or adolescent if he or she is feeling depressed and suicidal. Have a young person with the signs in Table 2 see the family physician immediately. There are good treatments for depression

TABLE 2

**Depression: Some Possible Warning Signs:**

---

Poor Appetite

Poor Concentration

Depressed Mood

Feelings of Guilt

Feelings of Hopelessness

Loss of Libido

Diminished Sense of Pleasures

Sleep Disturbances

Suicidal Thoughts or Plans

Weight Loss

Worthlessness/Low Self-Esteem

---

in adolescents and for any suicidal thoughts or plans that may accompany such depression.

*The Media.* Finally, parents will want to monitor the impact of the media on their children's growth in these violent times. While the government can develop national policies to curtail violence and while the industry can attempt to police itself, there is no substitute for parental supervision. Teach your child to be media literate by helping your child understand the meaning of the programming. What does the violence mean, what does it do to the victims, and what are alterna-tives to resolving the problem in nonviolent ways? Parents may also want to come together in advocacy groups to influence governmental policy, to organize boycotts and the like, but day-to-day monitoring and correcting the false messages is truly necessary.

This section has outlined basic parental and childrearing considera-tions for the early childhood development of decent children who are socially adept, intellectually curious, and not predisposed to vio-lence. Although some of these tasks are familiar, we do not want to underestimate their importance. As familiar as they are, the statistics on youth crime that we noted in chapter 1 suggest that many chil-dren still have not mastered these basic academic and social skills.

# Schools

## *Strengthening Community: Basic Approaches*

Society looks to its schools to strengthen the development of the child that has begun at home so that our young people mature into productive, socially responsible citizens. Time and again we have noted the importance of education in the postindustrial state. Education is important to all of us in terms of our national strength in a competitive global economy as well as to us individually in terms of adequate employment and a decent quality of life for our children and our grandchildren. As long as children in other parts of the world are better educated than our own citizens, earned income will reside in those other countries, the permanent underclass will continue to grow at home, and we can expect violence and crime to persist. As a nation, it is in our interest to address the issues related to adequate schooling. We need to draw upon the resources of administrators, teachers, teachers' unions, parents, and citizens who may no longer have school-age children as we attempt to improve our national quality of education.

*Standards.* There are many possible ways to strengthen our-selves academically. The first is to pool our created energies and resources in developing curricula that are tailored to the needs of the emerging knowledge-based state and the service system need-ed to support it. We need to move beyond the Taylor curriculum that trains students for industrial jobs that no longer exist, and focus on courses that teach computer literacy and the intellectu- al skills needed for the analytic thinking required for research and development.

The development of national standards is a second approach that many are considering. The standards would contain a basic mini- mum level of educational attainment, and would require that no stu- dent be allowed to graduate until that student has mastered the basic skills needed to be a productive citizen. Some states such as Arkansas, Louisiana, North Carolina, South Carolina, and Virginia already have promotional exams of some form. The country could follow these examples and develop national exams for elementary, middle, and high schools as other countries do. These exams might contain different standards for those bound for college versus those bound for vocational and trade careers, but either would address the need for some minimum standard of competence for each citizen.

A third method of improving academic excellence being con- sidered by several states is the use of a parent voucher system. A school district determines how much money is allotted for the education of each child. The parent is then given a voucher for that dollar amount, and can choose which school his or her child should attend. Various proposals include choices of public schools, religious schools, private schools, or some combination of these groupings. This approach is meant to reward good schools and to introduce some element of competition into the education system on the assumption that this will increase the overall level of quality over time. Although this approach has some merit, consideration needs to be given to those children who may remain in the less adequate school programs. Without ade- quate resources, the possibility of learning the basic skills needed for the postindustrial state is reduced. Both they as individuals and society as a whole will not benefit if they graduate into the permanent underclass.

A fourth possible approach to improving academic standards is to encourage business, colleges, and universities to become actively involved in improving the quality of education in local public schools. These organizations can be helpful in providing faculty to enhance the education of the classroom teachers and even to teach courses directly. Their presence enhances interest in the real world of business and employment or provides incentive motivation for higher education.

These suggestions are by no means exhaustive of the possibilities, and other creative solutions are being fielded. What is common to all of these approaches is an awareness of the importance of some basic standard of academic attainment for our children.

*Physical Plant and Supplies.* Students cannot be expected to do their best work in facilities that are unsafe and that lack basic resources. Although many affluent suburbs have adequate resources, many more urban, suburban, and rural settings do not. The problem is further complicated by a growing reluctance of the citizenry to provide extra school funding requests by means of increased taxes.

Since dollars are scarce, basic business practices of fiscal awareness may be of value to school systems. Here the private business sector might provide needed expertise in advising principals and school boards in sound financial planning. In addition, the private sector might also provide some form of direct financial assistance. Consider the following example. The Harriet Tubman School is located in a low-income neighborhood of Newark, New Jersey, but its students excel academically. Much of this has been accomplished with money from private foundations. Over the years, these funds have been used to train parents in how to read to their children; to purchase computers, science, and video equipment for academics; and to provide musical instruments for social and recreational purposes. This is a good example of the potentially creative solutions from the public education/private foundation interface.

*Teachers.* Teachers are clearly pivotal figures in our collective efforts to improve the quality of education nationally. Teachers have a complicated mission, and deserve the support of all of us in a variety of ways to ensure their success.

To begin with, it seems unreasonable to expect teachers to perform all of the social roles that we noted earlier. Although many attempt in good faith to be parental surrogates, nurses, policemen and the like, these other roles take time from the basic mission of teaching and creative thinking is needed on how to free teachers from these nonacademic roles. Greater parental involvement, adult volunteers, and the emerging role of the school as a one-step health delivery system (see below) are all helpful beginnings in this regard.

Teachers also need our assistance in strengthening their academic roles. This includes time to prepare relevant curricula and to maintain proficiency in their subject area, and school systems have developed a number of creative ways to provide teachers with these opportunities for continuing education in this era of rapid postindustrial change. These academic efforts are greatly enhanced if the school system has adopted policies that foster learning. Policies of zero tolerance for weapons, for substance abuse, and for violence in the building or on school grounds enable teachers and students to feel safe and then to concentrate on academic matters.

*Academics.* The academic deficiencies that we have noted earlier suggest the need for students in the postindustrial period to have a thorough grounding in English, math, general science, and computer literacy. A working knowledge of literature and history are also helpful to students as these bodies of knowledge show us how people deal with pain, suffering, and death; how societies prevent people from behaving in aggressive and greedy ways; and how these same societies utilize law and morality to enhance the meaning of life. These subjects teach the student to make informed choices, an important skill in the knowledge-based society.

Schools are developing creative solutions to enhance academics for the knowledge-based society. Some states like Georgia, South Carolina, and Texas have begun to emphasize early childhood education at the preschool level for children at risk and have developed a variety of programs to teach basic academic and social skills. Georgia has gone one step further and provides free preschool education to all of its four-year-olds. Early results are encouraging. For example, those who have been in the preschool program in Georgia score higher academically than those without schooling.

Other programs have been developed to meet the needs of older students. For example, based on the assumption that the school is the hub of its communities, Chicago opens two-thirds of its public schools for the summer. Summer programs include academics, art, music, tutoring, and recreational programs. This is a creative approach to the needs of students in the summer and also increases the total number of school days spent in preparation for the postindustrial economy.

Schools have approached the problem of declining parental involvement in recent years in equally creative ways. Some school districts have parent advisory boards for hiring, curriculum development, and drafting policies on violence and drugs and other school matters. In this way, parents have a voice in their children's academic needs. For example, parents have been a force in creating alternative schools to ensure that students receive an adequate education. Maine now has the Maine School of Science and Math for junior and senior high school students who wish to specialize in these areas. Chelsea, Massachusetts, parents joined with the faculty from Boston University in creating an intergenerational reading program. In this joint effort, parents keep a portfolio of what their children read, and the faculty help parents teach their children the skills of understanding the setting, problem, solutions, and consequences of each story. In the Williamsburg section of Brooklyn, New York, when the drop-out rate became unacceptably high, the community created the El Puente Academy for Peace and Justice to reach out to students from a different cultural background. These examples of constructive parental involvement channel creative parental energies into traditional school programs with beneficial outcomes for the students and their families.

*After School.* Since most juvenile violent crime occurs after school, the community benefits if its schools do not remain closed at the end of the school day. These buildings are potentially an important community resource for addressing the needs of our youth and for curbing violence.

When school is not in session, the school provides a community locale and set of resources for needed community activities. Recreational programs can be conducted for youth. Drop-in centers can be created to provide social support to substance abusers in treatment, for single mothers needing training in parental skills, for support and retraining for laid-off adult employees, for senior citizens, for youth to hang out and the like. These programs are not meant to provide additional responsibilities for teachers and would be run by specialists in each area of need.

Health care provides an interesting example of the school's potential as a resource. Health care reform with its recent emphasis on the highest quality of care in the most cost-effective setting has led to service integration in many health care settings. A similar need to cut costs in education settings is leading to the emergence of a school-based one-stop health care delivery center. In one school setting, children and their parents can address academic needs, physical and mental health needs, substance abuse treatment, and a variety of social services from a team of specialists already on site.

Consider these examples. In Memphis, counseling, substance abuse treatment, social services consultations as well as curriculum development, educational programs, and psychosocial evaluations can now be obtained in one stop at school. Texas is starting its "Schools of the Future" program, which integrates health and human services with educational needs. Active involvement of parents, teachers, and public and private community organizations is expected. In Kentucky, when the state legislature reformed educational standards statewide, it also provided for the development of school-based Family Resources and Youth Services Centers. These centers can provide resources to families for coping with life stress, serious mental illness, substance abuse, and other needed social services.

These one-stop school-based health and social service programs provide needed resources and ease of access to parents who are busy and feeling overwhelmed, and they also provide a potential solution to the current problem of multiple roles for teachers. As resources become available in the school itself, students can be referred as need dictates. In this way, the school has become an important resource for each set of stakeholders, and augments the sense of community.

## Strengthening Community: Special Areas

In addition to teaching academics, schools need to further enhance the social skills of our young people and there are at least three sociological risk factors which could be actively addressed within the school community: substance abuse, weapons and violence, and discrimination.

*Substance Abuse.* Young people see drugs being bought and sold on the street and in their playgrounds and they have little information with which to make reasonable judgments. Children and adolescents need courses on drugs and what they can do to the body and one's ability to work and enjoy life. The message on the street is one of glamour, not of physical pain and violence. Although students need to learn to say NO, they also need to learn a set of verbal and behavioral skills that enable them to say NO in the face of considerable social pressure from drug dealers and peers. Role-playing how to say no with the skills necessary to implement this solution is one school approach that has proved helpful in many states.

*Violence.* School programs have also been developed to address violent behavior in its many forms. Many students do not feel safe in coming to school or in being in the building itself. Some even bring guns for self-defense, which only compounds the problem.

Metal detectors and security guards may help, but the presence of potentially violent students induces fear in many nonviolent young-sters and interferes with academic learning. School districts may wish to consider policies where the chronically violent students are educated in a separate setting.

School materials that present information on what violence is, what are the types of violence, what causes violence to escalate, its warning signs, and what can be done to de-escalate aggression before it occurs, are helpful. Such a curriculum provides the teacher with the opportunity to teach verbal conflict resolution skills, the difference between being assertive (stating clearly your needs in a way that invites cooperation) and being aggressive (attempting to fulfill your own needs at the expense of others by force or fraud), and to refine empathic skills. [See Hechinger (1994) for a recent review of effective programs in this regard.]

*Discrimination.* Finally, sensitivity training for understanding, appreciating, and tolerating the differences in others is an addition-al area where school training may be helpful. Helping students understand differences in terms of race, ethnicity, religion, gender, age, or physical hardship as well as what we all have in common reduces the fear of the unknown and enhances more cooperative behavior in the long term. Such training early on at home and rein-forced in school reduces the risk of scapegoating a group of people when times are difficult and resources are scarce, and may enhance group cohesiveness of all the members in the face of life stress.

## Religion

Religion has always been a central force in our country, but how are we to understand its place in an era of scientific advancement and the emergence of the postindustrial state that is built upon scientific advances? A brief explanation may be of help as we contemplate our technological advances.

*Overview.* In 1901–2, psychologist William James (1958) gave a series of lectures on religion at the University of Edinburgh in Scotland. Surveying the variety of possible religious experiences, he came to the following conclusions. First, he believed that the evidence showed that the visible, physical world is part of a larger spiritual universe. Second, he felt that union or harmony with that spiritual universe was the true goal of our life's activities and that this yearning was biologically rooted. Third, he stated that prayer was the pathway from this physical world to the spiritual universe. His studies and observations suggested to him that religious people had a new zest for life, and that religion provided believers with a sense of security, peace, and love for others. He was adamant in insisting that there were needs for differing religions, in that each people's histories and problems differed, but he was equally firm in the belief that science could not fill the void of religious experience because science dealt with the abstract and concrete whereas religion dealt with the personal aspects of experience.

Historians Will and Ariel Durant similarly have much to teach about the role of religion in a society such as ours. After having written several volumes that encompassed ten thousand years of human history, they wrote a small volume that distilled the lessons from history that they had learned (1968). Both morals and religion were considered.

Morals are the rules by which a society exhorts its members to behave so that the social order is preserved. As with William James, the Durants found that there were universal moral ethics that were altered at times by history and the environment. For example, the hunter-gatherers emphasized brutality, bellicosity, and sexual readiness to survive. This was replaced during the agricultural period of human history by the values of industriousness, thrift, and peace. During the industrial revolution, individualism and material gain again rose to the fore.

Religion emerges when these codes of morals are received from God. The belief in religion helps people who are suffering and are unhappy. It helps the bereaved. It gives dignity to the poor and disabled. It provides discipline for the young, and it can make human relationships sacred as it does in matrimony. Religion not only helps us understand joy, but it provides meaning in the face of pain, suffering, and death, issues over which science provides little solace.

The Durants came to conclusions similar to those of William James. Religion is important to society in that in all of history there is no significant example of a society maintaining an adequate moral order without religion. The differing needs of people require flexibility in the religious experience but science will never be an adequate substitute.

The Durants provide two additional lessons from history that are important in our own immediate age: (1) religion must prevail when laws are weak and the moral resolve of the people must maintain the social order and (2) war increases the moral laxity of any age.

Thus, the answer to our question is that religion does have an important role to play in an age of science. Its role takes on additional importance when we consider that ours is an age of enormous change based on technological advances and an age that has seen its share of wars.

That our understanding of religion is changing and evolving should neither surprise nor frighten us. Change in religion is part of American history. The colonial state churches gave rise to several Protestant denominations which in turn grew into a variety of religious experiences and faiths. In our current periods of change, the challenge is to retain the basic message of all of the world's great religions: a sacred concern for the welfare of others. Ernest Becker (1973) was correct when he cited a person's need to find transcendent meaning as a way of addressing one's own mortality. Concern for others was his suggestion for transcendence and remains an important goal for religion, and for believers in an age of crime and violence.

*Clergy.* The American Psychological Association recently reported on a survey of today's clergy. There were 225,000 Protestant ministers, 4,000 rabbis, and 53,000 Catholic priests. These clergy spend ten to twenty percent of their time in counseling activities for an estimated 148.2 million hours of counseling a year. Not included in the survey were clergy of other faiths and about 100,000 Roman Catholic nuns. Clearly, here is a powerful moral voice for society.

Their counseling activities include working with the young, preparing couples for marriage and parenting, visiting the sick and the disabled, consoling the dying and the bereaved, and working on community tasks to strengthen society. In each of these activities, the clerical voice can begin to foster caring attachments and strengthen community by addressing the moral decay and violence in society.

*Religious Format.* Sociologist Robert Wurthnow (1994) has documented the gradual emergence of a new form of worship, the small group. Four out of ten Americans now belong to a small group and many are in religious settings. Bible-study classes, the treatment of addictions, singles and divorced groups, parenting groups, educational and recreation groups for youth are methods being adopted by many of our citizens as a way of attaining a sense of individual belonging, emotional support, and companionship. It is as if society is developing its own new capacity to generate caring attachments and a sense of community in the face of the disruptions that have recently been encountered.

## Strengthening Community: Basic Approaches and Special Areas

Sustained by concern for others and working within the small-group format, the clergy are at work on many exciting projects that address the need for community as well as specific sociological risk factors. Following are some examples.

Since 1917, Father Flanagan's Boy's Town has been taking care of children in need. Expanding beyond its initial vision, the program now takes children of both genders and all creeds, races, and ethnic groups. It is family oriented in small residential homes, and includes emerging shelters and a national research hospital. Its focus for over 17,000 children has been and remains that of discipline, family, skills-based education, and religion.

Brandeis University has just completed its tenth year of a summer institute for teachers that instructs them in an antidiscrimination curriculum. Over 25,000 teachers have attended. In June of 1995, the Southern Baptist Convention, which broke away from the American Baptist Convention in defense of slavery over 150 years ago, formally renounced racism in any form.

Campus Ministries at Columbia University, Vanderbilt University, Boston University, and the University of Southern California, to name a few, have all strengthened their programs in response to university student demand. Mission Mississippi, funded by sixty local churches and major state-based corporations, has begun a racial program statewide to reduce discrimination and hatred.

Islam has begun several initiatives nationally. For example, in the East Germantown neighborhood of Philadelphia a mosque opened in 1992 that offers home-work associations, crime watches, a Big Brother program, and classes in computer programming and typing. Another recent religious development has been the growth of the megachurches, such as that of Las Colinas in Irving, Texas. These churches may have anywhere from 3,000 to 15,000 members, but the emphasis is on an array of small groups to make members of the congregations feel part of the community.

More recently, many churches have also become very active in economic issues in pressing for workers' rights. Banding together with labor unions and community development groups, they have begun to address the needs of the permanent underclass by seeking just wages at a poultry-processing plant in North Carolina, in starting an employee-owned health care company in Connecticut, and in assisting employees in buying firms close to bankruptcy in Massachusetts.

As with parenting and schools, there are as many potential creative solutions as there are clergy who undertake them. This chapter clearly indicates that the family, school, and religion remain powerful moral voices in which ordinary citizens and groups of citizens are making strides in containing violence and crime.

## Violence in America: Some Final Thoughts

We have seen how periods of great social change, such as the one we are now experiencing in the postindustrial state, require our major societal institutions (business, government, the family, school, and religion) to change and that the guidelines for acceptable behavior from these institutions change as the institutions themselves are altered. Caring attachments are disrupted, the sense of community is weakened, and anomie is pervasive. During such a period, the other risk factors for violence are exacerbated. In our own age we are seeing increased biological risk factors in hyperreactive states, increased sociological risk factors in poverty, domestic violence, discrimination, inadequate schooling, substance abuse, and violence in the media, and increased psychological risk factors in faulty mastery and faulty meaning based on injustice and evil choices.

However, we have also learned that we are not helpless in the face of this national public health problem, that we are not a "traumatized society" as some would suggest. We have seen an array of approaches by ordinary citizens and professionals that contain and reduce violence by strengthening caring attachments and the sense of community as well as by addressing specific sociological risk factors. Just as the risk factors can contribute individually and interactively to increased crime, the remedial intervention of citizens individually and collectively can decrease crime. Americans have been successful with this problem in the past, and we can be so again.

Some will say that this will not be easy. This is true. People who are violent and commit crimes will not quickly stop. It will require the persistent efforts of each of us to strengthen the moral voice of concern for others in our societal institutions.

Some will say that we should start with the very young. This is true. The sooner we create caring attachments for the country's children, and teach them that rights carry with them responsibilities toward others, the more quickly will societal violence subside.

Some will say that this is hard to do alone. This is also true. None of us can solve this problem alone. We need to choose an area to address that is consistent with our skills and interests and then seek out others who have the same concerns. In this process, we shall be forming small groups and developing with each other the caring attachments that strengthen our communities and minimize the negative effects of anomie.

Some will say that ours is an age of cynicism and that citizens will not come forward. This is not true. Even in an age of personal entitlement, there remain citizens who want to help others. Each week presents examples of such men and women participating in neighborhood environmental clean-ups, engaging in walks and marathons for special charities, serving meals to the elderly and homeless, and so forth. The volunteer spirit in America remains. The desire for community is present.

Initiatives now exist to reduce violent crime. A lasting tragedy would occur if the information in these pages was not put to use. Many of us have an understandable reluctance to become involved or the desire to leave it to the next person. The result of these approaches will be a continuing spiral of crime and violence. A better strategy is for each of us to invest our energies in one small, manageable aspect of the problem. This personal commitment by each of us will ultimately reduce the violence in our homes, in our worksites, and in our communities.

The challenge to create communities that are safe and responsive, for ourselves and for our children, is before us. Together, let us take back the night.

# APPENDIX A

# Studies of Offenders:
# Select Scientific References

Aichorn, A. *Wayward Youth*. New York: The Viking Press, 1935.

Alhstrom, W., and Havighurst, R. *Four Hundred Losers: Delinquent Boys in High School*, San Francisco: Jossey-Bass, 1971.

Glueck, S. and E. *Five Hundred Career Criminals*. New York: 1939. New York: Kraus Reprints, 1975.

Glueck, S. and E. *Five Hundred Delinquent Women*. New York: 1934. New York: Kraus Reprints, 1971.

Glueck, S. and E. *Juvenile Delinquents Grown-Up*. New York: The Commonwealth Fund, 1940.

Glueck, S. and E. *Unraveling Juvenile Delinquency*. Cambridge, MA: Harvard University Press, 1950.

Harris, M. "Aggression, Gender, and Ethnicity." *Aggression and Violent Behavior*, 1 (1996): 123-146.

Konopka, G. *The Adolescent Girl in Conflict*. Englewood Cliffs, NJ: Prentice-Hall, 1966.

McCord, W., and McCord, J., with Zola, I. *Origins of Crime: A New Evaluation of the Cambridge-Somerville Youth Study*. New York: Columbia University Press, 1959.

Powers, E., and Witmer, H. *An Experiment in the Prevention of Delinquency: The Cambridge-Somerville Youth Study*. New York: Columbia University Press, 1951.

Redl, F., and Wineman, D. *Children Who Hate: The Disorganization and Breakdown of Behavior Controls*. New York: The Free Press, 1951.

Robins, L. Deviant *Children Grown Up: A Sociological and Psychiatric Study of Sociopathic Personality*. Baltimore: Williams and Wilkins, 1966.

Simmons, R., and Landis, J. *The Crimes Women Commit, The Punishments They Receive*. Lexington, Mass.: Lexington Books, 1991.

Tracy, P., Wolfgang, M. E., and Figlio, R. M. *Delinquency Careers in Two Birth Cohorts*. New York: Plenum Press, 1990.

Wolfgang, M. E., Figlio, R. M., and Sellin, T. *Delinquency in a Birth Cohort*. Chicago: University of Chicago Press, 1972.

# APPENDIX B

# National Associations in Reducing Violence: Select Listing

Listed below is a representative sample of national associations and societies that are interested in reducing violence. They are listed by topics, and the reader should feel free to contact these groups for information or direction. This listing is by no means exhaustive of the possibilities available to citizens. Similar state and municipal organizations may be found in local telephone directories.

## Counseling Societies

American Nurses Association
600 Maryland Avenue, SW
Suite 100 West
Washington, DC 20024

American Psychiatric Association
1400 K Street, NW
Washington, DC 20005

National Association
of Social Workers
750 First Street, NE
Washington, DC 20002

American Psychological
Association
750 First Street, NE
Washington, DC 20002

## Crime

American Correctional
Association
8025 Laurel Lakes Court
Laurel, MD 20707

National Crime Prevention
Council
1700 K Street, NW
Washington, DC 20006

Federal Bureau of Investigation
10th Street and Pennsylvania
Ave., NW
Washington, DC 20535

National Criminal Justice Assn.
444 Capitol Street, NW
Suite 618
Washington, DC 20001

National Council on Crime
and Delinquency
685 Market Street/Suite 620
San Francisco, CA 94105

U.S. Department of Justice
Criminal Division
Main Justice Building
Washington, DC 20530

## *Discrimination*

American Civil Liberties Union
Foundation (ACLU)
1875 Connecticut Ave., NW
Washington, DC 20009

NAACP Legal Defense and
Educational Fund
1275 K. Street, NW, #301
Washington, DC 20005

Antidefamation League
of B'nai B'rith
823 United Nations Plaza
New York, NY 10017

National Institute Against
Prejudice and Violence
31 South Greene Street
Baltimore, MD 21201

## *Education*

American Federation
of Teachers
555 New Jersey Avenue, NW
Washington, DC 20001

National Education Assn
1201 16th Street, NW
Washington, DC 20036

Council of Chief State
Schools Officers
1 Massachusetts Avenue, NW
Washington, DC 20001

U.S. Department of
Education
600 Independence Ave., SW
Washington, DC 20002

## *Guns/Weapons*

American Bar Association
1800 M Street, NW
Washington, DC 20035

Gun Owners of America
8001 Forbes Place
Suite 102
Springfield, VA 22151

Center to Prevent
Handgun Violence
1225 I Street, NW, Suite 1100
Washington, DC 20005

National Rifle Association
1600 Rhode Island Ave., NW
Washington, DC 20036

## Media

Center for Media and
Public Affairs
2101 L Street, NW,
Washington, DC 20037

Morality in Media
475 Riverside Drive
Suite 405
New York, NY 10115

Free Press Association
P.O. Box 15548
Columbus, OH 43215

National Council for Families
and Television
3801 Barkam Boulevard
Suite 300
Los Angeles, CA 90068

## Substance Abuse

Alcoholics Anonymous (AA)
P.O. Box 459
Grand Central Station
New York, NY 10163

National Federation of
Parents for Drug-Free Youth
8730 Georgia Avenue
Suite 200
Silver Spring, MD 20910

Al-Anon Family Group
Headquarters
1372 Broadway
New York, NY 10018

National Institute on Alcohol
Abuse and Alcoholism
(NIAAA)
Room 16-105,
Parklawn Building
5600 Fishers Lane
Rockville, MD 20857

Narcotics Anonymous
World Service Office, Inc.
P.O. Box 999
Van Nuys, CA 91409

National Institute on
Drug Abuse (NIDA)
Room 10-05,
Parklawn Building
5600 Fisher Lane
Rockville, MD 20857

## Youth Violence

Center for Study of Youth Policy
University of Michigan
School of Social Work
1015 Huron Street
Ann Arbor, MI 48104

National School Safety
Center
4165 Thousand Oaks Blvd
Suite 290
Westlake Village, CA 91362

Mothers Against Gangs
110 W. Madison Street
Chicago, IL 60602

U.S. Department of Justice
Juvenile Justice and
Delinquency Prevention
633 Indiana Avenue, NW
Washington, DC 20531

National Council of Juvenile
and Family Court Judges
P.O. Box 8970
University of Nevada
Reno, NV 89557

U.S. Drug Enforcement
Administration
1405 I Street, NW
Washington, DC 20537

## Victims of Violence

International Society for
Stress Traumatic Studies
435 N. Michigan Avenue
Suite 1717
Chicago, IL 60640

National Organization for
Victim Assistance
1757 Park Road, NW
Washington, DC 20010

C.H. Kempe National Center for
Prevention andTreatment
of Child Abuse
1205 Oneida Avenue
Denver, CO 80220

National Victim Center
309 West 7th Street
Suite 705
Fort Worth, TX 76102

National Coalition Against
Domestic Violence
P.O. Box 34103
Washington, DC 20043

Parents of Murdered Children
100 East 8th Street
Cincinnati, OH 45202

# Select Readings

## Chapter 1: It's the Nature of the Times: Cultural Factors in Violence

Derber, C. *The Wilding of America. How Greed and Violence are Eroding Our Nation and Character.* New York: St. Martin's Press, 1996.

Dobrin, A., Wiersema, B., Loftin, C., and McDowall, D. *Statistical Handbook of Violence in America.* Phoenix, AZ: Ornyx Press, 1996.

Drucker, P. "The Age of Social Transformation." *Atlantic Monthly,* 276 (1994), 53-80.

Durkheim, É. *Suicide: A Study in Sociology.* Trans: J. Spaulding and G. Simpson. New York: The Free Press, 1951.

Flannery, R. B., Jr. *Violence in the Workplace.* New York: Crossroad, 1995.

Gordon, O. *Fat and Mean: The Corporate Squeeze of Working Americans and the Managerial "Myth" of Downsizing.* New York: Free Press, 1996.

Madrick, J. *The End of Affluence: The Causes and Consequences of America's Economic Decline.* New York: Random House, 1995.

Messner, S. F., and Rosenfeld, R. *Crime and the American Dream.* Belmont, CA: Wadsworth Publishing, 1994.

National Research Council. *Understanding and Preventing Violence.* Washington, DC: National Academy Press, 1993.

Sorokin, P. A. *The Crisis of Our Age.* New York: Dutton, 1941.

Summer, C. *The Sociology of Deviance: An Obituary.* New York: Continuum, 1994.

Thurow, L. *The Future of Capitalism: How Today's Economic Forces Shape Tomorrow's World.* New York: Morrow, 1996.

## Chapter 2: Who in His Right Mind Would Do Such a Thing?: Biological Factors in Violence

Archer, J. (Ed.). *Male Violence.* New York: Routledge, 1994.

Ardrey, R. *The Territorial Imperative: A Personal Inquiry into the Animal Origins of Property and Nations.* New York: Atheneum, 1966.

Bouchard, T. J., Jr. "Genes, Environment, and Personality." *Science,* 264 (1994): 1700-1701.

Daly, M., and Wilson, M. *Homicide.* New York: Aldine DeGruyter, 1988.

de Waal, F. *Peacemaking Among Primates.* Cambridge, MA: Harvard University Press, 1989.

Lorenz, K. Trans: Wilson, M. K. *On Aggression.* New York: Harcourt, Brace, and World, Inc., 1963.

Montagu, A. (Ed.) *Man and Aggression.* 2nd Edition. New York: Oxford University Press, 1973.

Montagu, A. (Ed.) *Learning Non-Aggression: The Experience of Non-Literate Societies.* New York: Oxford, 1978.

Morris, D. *The Naked Ape: A Zoologist's Study of the Human Animal.* New York: McGraw Hill, 1967.

Schachter, S., and Singer, J. "Cognitive, Social, and Physiological Determinants of Emotional State." *Psychological Review* 69 (1962): 379-399.

Whiteford, M. B., and Friedle, J. *The Human Portrait: Introduction to Cultural Anthropology.* 3rd Edition. Englewood Cliffs, NJ: Prentice Hall, 1992.

Wilson, E. O. *Sociobiology: The New Synthesis.* Cambridge, MA: Harvard University Press, 1975.

## Chapter 3: No Man Is an Island: Sociological Factors in Violence

Bowlby, J. *Attachment and Loss, Vol. I: Attachment.* New York: Basic Books, 1973.

Flannery, R. B., Jr. *Becoming Stress-Resistant Through the Project SMART Program.* New York: Continuum, 1990. Paperback, New York: Crossroad, 1994.

Flannery, R. B., Jr. *Post-Traumatic Stress Disorder: The Victim's Guide to Healing and Recovery.* New York: Crossroad, 1992. Paperback: 1994.

Goldstein, A. *Addiction: From Biology to Drug Policy.* New York: Freeman, 1994.

Harlow, H., and Mears, C. *The Human Model: Private Perspectives.* New York: Wiley, 1979.

Kagan, J., and Zentner, M. "Early Childhood Predictors of Adult Psychopathology." *Harvard Review of Psychiatry* 3 (1996): 341-350.

Lynch, J. *The Broken Heart: The Medical Consequences of Loneliness.* New York: Basic Books, 1977.

Prendergast, C. *Sexual Abuse of Children and Adolescents: A Preventive Guide for Parents, Teachers and Counselors.* New York: Continuum, 1996.

Sagan, L. N. *The Health of Nature: True Cases of Sickness and Well-Being.* New York: Basic Books, 1987.

Verny, T. with Keller, J. *The Secret Life of the Unborn Child.* New York: Summit, 1981.

Widom, C. S. "The Cycle of Violence." *National Institute of Justice: Research in Grief.* October (1992): 1-6.

Wilson, P. *Children Who Kill.* London: Michael Joseph, Ltd., 1973.

## Chapter 4: In the Eye of the Beholder: Psychological Factors in Violence

Antonovsky, A. *Health, Stress, and Coping.* San Francisco: Jossey-Bass, 1979.

Becker, E. *The Denial of Death.* New York: Free Press, 1973.

Darwin, C. *The Origin of the Species.* New York: Modern Library Edition, 1995.

Eron, L. D., Gentry, J. H., and Schlegel, P. (Eds.) *Reason to Hope: A Psychological Perspective on Violence and Youth.* Washington, DC: American Psychological Association, 1994.

Foster, C., Siegel, M., and Landes, A. *Education—Reflecting on Our Society?* Wylie, TX: Information Plus, 1994.

Gilligan, J. *Violence: Our Deadly Epidemic and Its Causes.* New York: Putnam, 1996.

Hall, C. S., and Lindzey, G. *Theories of Personality.* New York: Wiley, 1957.

Huesman, L. R. *Aggressive Behavior: Current Perspectives.* New York: Plenum Press, 1994.

Justice, B. *Who Gets Sick: How Beliefs, Moods, and Thoughts Reflect Your Behavior.* Los Angeles: J. P. Tarcher, 1988.

Milgram, S. "Behavioral Study of Obedience." *Journal of Abnormal and Social Psychology* 67 (1963): 371-378.

Scherer, K. R., Abeles, R. B., and Fischer, C. S. *Human Aggression and Conflict: Interdisciplinary Perspectives.* Englewood, NJ: Prentice-Hall, 1975.

Toch, H. *Violent Men: An Inquiry into the Psychology of Violence.* Rev. Ed. Washington, DC: American Psychological Association, 1992.

## Chapter 5: Restoring Community: Business and Government

Biskup, M. D., and Cozic, C. P. (Eds.) *Youth Violence: Current Controversies.* San Diego: Greenhaven Press, 1992.

Cozic, C. *Gun Control: Current Controversies.* San Diego: Greenhaven Press, 1992.

Fortune, M. *Love Does No Harm: Sexual Ethics for the Rest of Us.* New York: Continuum, 1995.

Gottfredson, M. R., and Hirschi, T. A *General Theory of Crime.* Stanford, CA: Stanford University Press, (1990).

Guggenbühl, A. *The Incredible Fascination of Violence: Ideas on Dealing with Aggression and Brutality Among Children.* Woodstock, CT: Spring, 1996.

Kapstein, E. B. "Workers and the World Economy." *Foreign Affairs* 75 (1996): 16-37.

Katz, J. *Seductions of Crime: Mood and Sensual Attractions in Doing Evil.* New York: Basic Books, 1988.

Khantzian, E. "The Self-Medication Hypothesis of Affective Disorders: Focus on Heroin and Cocaine Addiction." *American Journal of Psychiatry,* 142 (l985): 1259-64.

Kortin, D. C. *When Corporations Rule the World.* West Hartford, CT: Kumarian and San Francisco, CA: Barrett-Koehler, 1995.

Kozol, J. *Savage Inequalities: Children in America's Schools.* New York: Crown, 1991.

Reichheld, F. F. with Teal, T. *The Loyalty Effect: The Hidden Face Behind Growth, Profits and Lasting Value.* Cambridge, MA: Harvard Business School Press, 1996.

Sandel, M. J. *America in Search of a Public Philosophy.* Cambridge, MA: Harvard University Press, 1996.

## Chapter 6: Restoring Community: Family, School, and Religion

Adams, C. J., and Fortune, M. (Eds.) *Violence against Women and Children: A Christian Theological Sourcebook.* New York: Continuum, 1995.

Durant, W. and A. *The Lessons of History.* New York: Simon and Schuster, 1968.

Etzioni, A. *The Spirit of Community: Rights, Responsibilities, and the Communitarian Agenda.* New York: Crown, 1993.

Godfred, N. S. with Richards, T. *A Penny-Saved: Using Money to Teach Young Children the Way the World Works.* New York: Simon and Schuster, 1995.

Hechinger, F. "Saving Youth from Violence." *Carnegie Quarterly* 39 (1994): Whole.

James, W. *The Varieties of Religious Experience.* New York: New American Library of World Literature, 1958.

Popenoe, D. *Life Without Father: Compelling New Evidence that Fatherhood and Marriage are Indispensible for the Good of Children and Society.* New York: Free Press, 1996.

Ryan, E. A. *Straight Talk About Drugs and Alcohol.* (Rev. Ed.) New York: Facts on File, 1995.

Silverberg, J., and Gray, P. (Eds.) *Aggression and Peacefulness in Humans and Other Primates.* New York: Oxford University Press, 1992.

Wechesser, C. *Violence in the Media: Current Controversies.* San Diego: Greenhaven Press, 1995.

Wise, F. H. *Youth and Drugs: Prevention, Detection, and Cure.* New York: Association Press, 1971.

Wurthnow, R. *Sharing the Journey: Support Groups for America's New Quest for Community.* New York: Free Press, 1994.

# Index

# About the Author

Raymond B. Flannery, Jr., Ph.D., a licensed clinical psychologist, is on the faculties of Harvard Medical School in Boston and the University of Massachusetts Medical Center in Worcester. For over twenty-five years, he has been a counselor and professional educator of businesspersons, professionals, health care providers, and the general public about life stress, psychological trauma, and violence in the community and in the workplace. He has lectured nationally and is the author of more than fifty-five papers in medical and science journals.

Dr. Flannery is also the author of three books for the general public and interested professionals. *Becoming Stress-Resistant through the Project SMART Program* (New York: Continuum, 1990; Crossroad, 1994) is for those wanting to learn how to cope effectively with the general stress of life. It is based on a twelve-year study of 1,200 persons and explores how the most adaptive among them coped with life stress. His second book, *Post-Traumatic Stress Disorder: The Victim's Guide to Healing and Recovery* (New York: Crossroad, 1992, 1994), is the first book written for victims of psychological trauma, and outlines effective coping strategies for persons seeking to recover from the severe stress of traumatic events. *Violence in the Workplace* (New York: Crossroad, 1995) is his third book. It is the first to examine the general nature and causes of worksite violence, and the first to present a threefold approach to reduce the risk of its occurrence and to contain its aftermath when it does occur.

Dr. Flannery and his wife live in the suburbs of Boston.

PUBLISHED BY CONTINUUM

Carol J. Adams and Marie M. Fortune, editors
*VIOLENCE AGAINST WOMEN AND CHILDREN*
*A Christian Theological Sourcebook*

"If you read only one book this year, let it be this one. . . . "
—*National Catholic Reporter*

Raymond B. Flannery, Jr., Ph.D.
*VIOLENCE IN AMERICA*
*Coping with Drugs, Distressed Families, Inadequate Schooling, and Acts of Hate*

"In this academic but accessible overview of violence, clinical psychologist Flannery (*Post-Traumatic Stress Disorder: The Victim's Guide to Healing and Recovery*) presents an impressive array of sociological studies and crime statistics to support his contention that violence in the U.S. has become a major public-health problem 'of epidemic proportion.' He argues convincingly that to slow the rate of violence, our major institutions must contribute to a solution."
—*Publishers Weekly*

Sigmund Freud
*PSYCHOLOGICAL WRITINGS AND LETTERS*

Edited by Sander L. Gilman, this volume includes: "Infant Sexuality," "Psychopathology of Everyday Life," "The Uncanny," "A Difficulty in the Path of Psychoanalysis," and other important works.

Hermann Langbein
*AGAINST ALL HOPE*
*Resistance in the Nazi Concentration Camps 1938–1945*

"A monumental study. Langbein's committment to truth is the greatest honor one could render to the memory of those who under the worst sufferings did not stop the fight for freedom."
—*La Monde*

William E. Prendergast, Ph.D.
*SEXUAL ABUSE OF CHILDREN AND ADOLESCENTS*
*A Preventive Guide for Parents, Teachers, and Counselors*

"Dr. Prendergast's helping method is pragmatic rather than being based on a particular model. It is somewhat reminiscent of Glasser's Reality Therapy in its directness and wise use of confrontation."
—Alan Keith-Lucas, Ph.D.

---

Juliet Cassuto Rothman
*THE BEREAVED PARENTS' SURVIVAL GUIDE*

"This book is beautifuly written. The insights shared here will bring comfort, strength, and hope to bereaved parents everywhere, in each of their many stages of grief. Juliet gives you the ability to believe that you will once again enjoy being part of mainstream life. Thank you, Juliet."
—Janet Tyler, bereaved parent and chapter leader of Bereaved Parents, U.S.A.

---

Colin Sumner
*THE SOCIOLOGY OF DEVIANCE*
*An Obituary*

"Sumner's book is well written and should have broad appeal. On the one hand, it is a rich and illuminating critique from within the community of practitioners in the sociology of deviance. On the other, it is an intellectual history that examines the linkages between a body of knowledge and the social world that it serves."
—*Canadian Journal of Criminology*

*At your bookstore or order from*
*The Continuum Publishing Company*
*370 Lexington Avenue*
*New York, NY 10017*

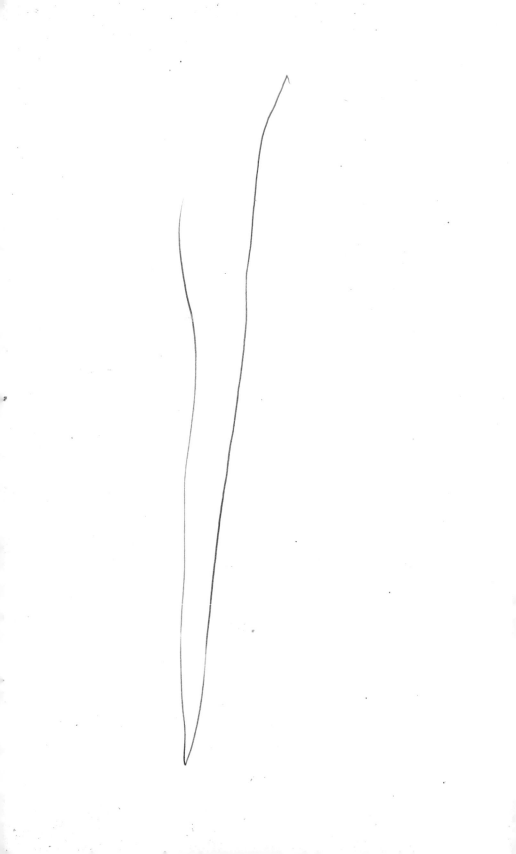